The Triumph of Death 1990

Stephen W Sweigart

ISBN 978-1-959895-35-0 (paperback)
ISBN 978-1-959895-34-3 (ebook)

Printed in the United States of America

THE INVOCATION TO THE TRIUMPH OF DEATH

I shall attempt only what immortals of Parnassus have achieved
Ye Gods of Greece, what invokes the Muses to be reborn
In this mortal framework, that I will attempt this great mechanization.

THE ARGUMENT OF THE TRIUMPH OF DEATH

The Second Great War, I descry, I preclude the Third.
How mankind slaughtered, by one man, bred.
How blood drenched Europe, and the Orient.

Of a small band of men, who resisted Capitalist suppression
And liquidation, In the State of New Jersey
And of how the foundation of a free State was conceived
The evolvement of European Socialist Republics.

AND ALL MEN SHALL HATE EACH OTHER.

SHALL THE POEM COMMENCE?

'THE LIQUIDATION OF CZECHOSLOVAKIA'

Hitler's recommendation to his staff:
Demands
should be made to the Sudeten German Party
Which are unacceptable to the Czech government.

President Emil Hacha
traveled
to Berlin:
received all formal honors
at the train station,
a bouquet of flowers
was presented to his daughter,
and chocolates.
a personal gift from Hitler.

The President had recently been informed that
German troops
occupied
Moravska-Ostrava
an important industrial town,
and positioned along the perimeter
of Bohemia and Moravia.
'The position of Resistance
would be folly. . .
he saw dawning the possibility
of a long period
of peace between two people'.
(Hacha to Hitler)
Yet he

refused to sign any documents
of surrender.
The German ministers warned
that Prague would be bombed
in a matter of hours.
Hacha fainted.
Hitler's doctors
injected him
and he regained consciousness.
Emil Hacha
telephoned
the Czech cabinet of the surrender.

'The safeguarding of calm, order, and peace
In thus part of Central Europe'.

Children! This is greatest day of my Life.
I shall go down as greatest German!
(Hitler)

CZECHOSLOVAKIA has ceased TO EXIST!
(Hitler)

Hitler slept in Hradschin Castle,
he declared:
'Autonomy and Self-Government'.

Miklos Horthy, Military elected regent of Hungary
Addressed Adolf Hitler
on 13 March:
'Your excellency: Heartfelt thanks!
On Thursday the 16th
a frontier incident will take place. . .'
le commencement de la fin

On 26 of August 1789, the Assembly adopted

'The Declaration of Human Rights of Man'.

The bourgeoisie representatives
Interest were primarily mercantile,
though they were influenced
by eighteenth-century
philosophers.
MIRABEAU: 'restrictions, and conditions which
in almost every instance
replace rights with obligations
fetters for liberty'.
LOUSTALOT: 'from the condition of slavery
to one of freedom,
but now we are marching
still more quickly from freedom
back to slavery.
That no one can be harassed
for his opinions, provided that

the expression of these opinions
does not disturb the order established
by law. This condition
is like a strap that stretches
And tightens at will.'
ROBESPIERRE: 'all privileges, distinctions,
and exceptions ought to disappear,
sovereignty rests in the people,
in every single individual
who is part of the mass populations.
Otherwise, it is simply not true
that men are equal in rights
and that every man is a citizen.'
MARAT: 'And so this system of representation,
by making political power
proportionate to the sum paid
in direct taxes,
will hand over control of the State
to the rich again,
and it will be impossible
for the poor, who are still oppressed
and kept in position
of subordination, to improve their lot,
by peaceful means.'
CAMILLE DESMOULINS:
'The capital is unanimous,
and soon the province will be
too, in their opposition
to the decree lying down

the property requirements
        for deputies.'
But what on earth is meant
        by the expression 'active citizens'
which we hear repeated so often?
Active citizens are men who stormed
                the bastille,
those that work the land,
        where as the idle members
                of the Court and Clergy,
despite the vast estates
        which they own, are
nothing than 'vegetables',
        vegetarian like that in scripture
which bore no fruit and which
                was therefore condemned
to be thrown into fire and burned.

The effect of the substance
        implanted that destroyed
my creativity could not be
                counteracted,
and only today has my creativity
        been restored.

Nietzsche spoke of the greatest joy
        developing out of
        of the greatest pain.

substance
DESTROYS
CREATIVITY

PAIN

22 September 1789, the assembly
    voted
that the 'government of France
            is monarchal'
The hereditary King of France
subordinate to the Constitution,
        yet the real power was controlled
by the property-owning
                middle classes,
        the moneyed groups
        which dominate
the economic life of the community.

Ist es schon so um mich bestellt.
Hat much Der schon dazu gemacht.
Auf! Schlagt die Feuerglocken drein!
Wer bin ich denn: Der reiche Jedermann.

CASE WHITE:

24 October, 1938, Ribbentrop hosted
ambassador, Jozef Lipski,
at a three-hour lunch
at the Grand Hotel in Berchtesgaden.
Poland had just seized a section
of Czechoslovakia Business:
'to speak to Poland about Danzig':
As well as the building
of a superhighway and double track
railroad across the border.
Hitler also desired Poland to form
an anti-Comintern Pact.
Lipski reminded Ribbentrop that
the Fuehrer had on two recent
occasions, 5 Nov, 1937 and 14 Jan. 1930,
assured the Polish people
he would not support any change
in Danzig Statute.
Colonel Beck, the Foreign Minister,
a week later, 31 October,
dispatched detailed instructions
to the ambassador in Berlin.

19, November, Ribbentrop
interviewed the ambassador,
'any attempt to incorporate the Free city

into the Reich, must inevitably
lead to conflict.'

TOP SECRET
preparations are also
to be made to enable
the Free State of Danzig
to be occupied by German troops
by surprise. Condition is quasi-revolutionary
occupation of Danzig, exploiting
a politically favorable situation,
not a war against Poland.'

'Danzig is German,
will always remain German,
and sooner or later become part of Germany.'
The reply of the Fuehrer
to Colonel Beck.

In 1922, General von Seeckt define
the situation:
'Poland's existence is intolerable.'
21, March 1939, Ribbentrop
met with Lipski, and explained
that the Fuehrer was becoming
amazed at Poland's attitude.
'Poland must realize that she could
not take a middle course
between Russia and Germany.'

Transport Exercise Stettin

'The Fuehrer would act with
                lightning speed
Ribbentrop explained to
Juozas Urbays, the Lithuanian
       Foreign Minister, unless
Lithuania returns the Memel district
              to Germany.
The German government had organized
        the Memel Germans.
Hitler and Admiral Raeder
abroad the battleship 'Deutschland',
       a day earlier, 21 March,
he had forewarned the Lithuanian
       government two days later,
Ribbentrop transmitted by radio
       that Lithuania had signed.
Hitler interpretated triumphantly
       and saluted 'liberated' Germans.

'The Fuehrer does not wish to solve
       Danzig problem by force.
He would not like to drive Poland
       into the hands of Great Britain'.
The persecution of the German Minority
              in Poland has created

'a disastrous impression on Germany'.
'of possible consequences.'
'it reminded him of certain risky steps
taken by another state'
'you want to negotiate at the point
of a bayonet! (Ribbentrop)
'this is your own method,' (Colonel Beck)
'If they expect Germany of today
to sit patiently by until the last day
while they create satellite States
and set them against Germany,
they are mistaking Germany of before the war. .
. . when they may in other countries
that they will arm and keep arming still more,
I can tell those statesmen only this:
'Me you will never tire out'
I am determined to continue
on this road,
'Germany has no intention attacking
other people. . . out of this conviction
I decided three weeks ago to name
the coming party rally the
Convention of Peace.'

28 April 1939, the Fuehrer answered
Roosevelt's 'policy of encirclement'

Mr. Roosevelt declares that it is clear
to him that all international problems

can be solved at the council table.
ANTWORT: . . . I would be very happy
If these problems could really find there
solution at the conference table.
My skepticism, however, is based
on the fact that it was America
herself that save the sharpest
conference of all time was
the League of Nations. . .
representing all peoples of the world.
Created in accordance with the will
of the American President.
The first State, however, that shrank
from the endeavor was the United States. . .
it was not until after years of purposeless
participation that I resolve
to follow the example of America.
GERMANY HAD ALREADY WENT TO
THE CONFERENCE TABLE AT VERSAILLES.
it's representatives 'WERE SUBJECTED TO
EVEN GREATER DEGRADATION
THEN EVER have been inflicted
on the chieftains of the Sioux tribes.'

TOP SECRET
1.   Political Requirements Aims. . .
The aim will be to destroy Polish military
strength and create in the East
a situation which satisfies the requirements

of national defense. . .The development
of increasing internal crisis in France
and the resulting British cautiousness
might produce such a situation
not to distant future.
2. Military Conclusions. The great
objective in building up of the German
armed forces will continue
to determine by the antagonisms
of the Western democracies.
3. Tasks of Armed Forces. The task of
the Wehrmacht is to destroy the Polish
armed forces. To this and
a surprise attack is to be aimed at
and prepared.

PREPARATIONS MUST BE MADE
IN SUCH A WAY IN THAT THE OPERATION
CAN BE CARRIED OUT AT ANY TIME
FROM 1 SEPTEMBER 1939, ONWARD.

6 April, Colonel Beck signed
an agreement
with Great Britain in London.
Mussolini sent troops into Albania
Goering arrived in Rome
and talked.
Mussolini: Roosevelt's appeal as

'a result of infantile paralysis,'

Goering disagreed: 'Roosevelt was
    suffering from an incipient
                mental disease.'

Finally, Mr. Roosevelt asks that assurance
            be given that the German
        armed forces will not attack,
            and above all, not invade
        the territory or possession
of the following independent nations. . .
    . . . are at present not in possession
of their freedom, but are occupied
        and consequently derived
            of their rights by military agents
of democratic States.

I here solemnly declare that all
        the assertions which have
            circulated In any way concerning
        an intended German attacks
            or invasion on or in American
                territory are rank frauds
                and gross untruths,
            quite apart from the fact.
    Mr. Roosevelt! I have conquered chaos
            in Germany, re-established
        order and enormous increase

In production. . . developed traffic . . .
and at the same time endeavored
to further the education
and culture of our people. . .
I have also endeavored
to destroy sheet by sheet that treaty. . .
I have brought back the Reich
provinces stolen from us in 1919
for me it is more precious
than anything else,
for it has limited to my people!. . .
the justice, well-being,
progress and peace
of the whole community.

Hitler transferred himself
to the mountain retreat
at Berchtesgaden.

Inaugural Address, January 20, 1981:
The business of the nation goes forward.
The United States are confronted with
economic affliction of great proportion.
We suffer from the longest and one of
the worst sustained inflations in our history.
It distorts our economic decisions,
penalizes thrift, and crushes the struggling
young and fixed elderly alike. It threatens

to shatter the lives of all our people. Idle industries have cast workers into unemployment, human misery, and personal indignity, those who do work are denied a fair return for their labor by a tax system which. . .

THE CAPITALIST MEDIA:
    THE ECONOMIC DOMINATION
    OF INFORMATION.
    THE CONTROL AND PROPAGATION
    OF COGNITION.

THE UNITED STATES SENATE, the silver charger,
    THE FINANCIAL SERVANT MOUNTED
    ON CORPORATE AND PERSONAL GREED.
    THE MANUFACTURERS OF MILITARY PROFIT,
    ULTIMATELY DESTRUCTIVE.
    PERSERVING A LEVEL OF TOLERANCE.
    A THESHOLD FOR THE PEOPLE.

CONCLUSION: THE END OF PART ONE.

AND ALL MEN SHALL HATE EACH OTHER.

EXCELLENT, YOU SHOULD NOW ATTEMPT A CRITIQUE!

PART TWO

STALIN; Iosif Vissarionovich Dzhugashvili,
opinion was that Western Allies
were pushing the Germans further
    eastward, promising them
the easy prey and saying: 'just start
    war with the Bolsheviks,
everything else will take care of itself'
        This looks much like encouragement. . .
STALIN'S PRINCIPLES
became:
1. To continue to pursue a policy of peace
and consolidation of economic relations
with all countries.
2. . . . Not to let our country be drawn into
conflict by warmongers, whose custom
it is to let others pull their chestnuts
out of the fire.

GOERING met MUSOLINI in Rome, 16 April.

IL Duce
replied: The object would be to induce Russia
to coolly and unfavorably to Britain's
efforts to settlement. . .'

THE PACT OF STEEL

Mussolini wished to avoid war
                at least for a few years.
Nor did the Wehrmacht think
              highly of the Italian military power.
Yet Hitler demanded
                a military alliance with Italy.

23, May
Hitler met with his military chiefs:
Further successes can no longer be attained
                without a shedding of blood.
Danzig is not the subject of the dispute
             at all. It is a question
          expanding our living space in the East,
              of securing our food supplies
           and also solving the problem
                of the Baltic States. . .
        There is no other possibility in Europe. . .
There is no question of sparing Poland
              and we are left with the decision:
To attack Poland at first suitable opportunity.
        We cannot expect a repetition
                of the Czech affair.
        There will be war.
           Our task is to isolate Poland.
        Success in isolating her will be decisive.

The aim must be to deal the enemy
        a smashing or a finally decisive blow
right at the start. . .
              Considerations of right or wrong
                     or of treaties
              do not enter into the matter. . .
Preparations must be made for a long war
           as well as for a surprise attack,
      and every possible intervention
by England on the continent
            must be smashed.
The army must occupy
        the positions of importance
for the fleet and Luftwaffe.
If we succeed in occupying Holland
         and Belgium,
      as well defeating France,
the basis for the successful war
         against England has been created.
The Luftwaffe can closely blockade
              with submarines.

Secrecy is the decisive prerequisite
                for success.
Our objective is to keep secret
        from Italy and Japan.

In the debate
In the HOUSE OF COMMONS, 19 May

CHURCHILL, backed by Lord George,
        argued that Moscow had made
            'a fair offer. . .more simple,
        more direct, more effective'

MOLOTOV gave his first speech
            as Commissar of Foreign Affairs:
The Western powers should JOIN
                the Soviet Union
        to stop AGGRESSION.

25 May,
Weizsaecker and Friedrich Gauss
            were summoned
        to Ribbentrop's country house
                at Sonnenburg,
        and were informed that the Fuehrer
            wanted 'to establish more tolerable
relations between Germany and Soviet Union'.

Weizsaecker said he agreed
        with Molotov that political
            and economic questions

could not be entirely separated
and expressed interest in 'normalization
of relations between Soviet Russia and Germany'.

30 May,
In a meeting with Georgi Astakhov,
Molotov requested that Great Britain
        send to Molotov

the Foreign Secretary:
William Stang, and official In the Foreign Office
arrived in Moscow on June 14,
        and participated in eleven
        Anglo-French meetings.

In Pravda
Andrei Zhdanov wrote,
'It seems to me, that British and French
        governments a real agreement
        acceptable to the U.S.S.R.
    but only talks about an agreement
    in order to demonstrate
        before the public opinion
        of their own countries
            the alleged unyielding
            attitude of U.S.S.R.'

Today, the first day of 1988,
  nine months
since the CHERRY HILL POLICE
  burst into my home,
before a rescheduled
  departure to Praha the DDR
A result of my brothers take over
  of the business, coupled with
the aftereffects
  of the MIND CONTROL DRUGS,
the State could no longer
  legally induce.
My brothers desired to guarantee
  their avid rights and
the capitalist business education
of learned misconceptions
  and delusions.
My opinions and intentions were
  discredited and
I was divested of my income.
I began to act on my views
  that only hence had been suppressed,
this deteriorated into mere speech
  and delusions.
I was then taken to a hospital
  after the police smashed
a window in my home, and transferred
  of my insurance arrangements
  to an upgraded hospital (rip-off)

Though at first semi-resistant
           within a few days
     no alternative existed:
                MIND CONTROL DRUGS.
                     I set in practice,
'my theory of deceptive cooperation'.

I was released in two and a half weeks,
yet forced overdose of mind controls,
Had a devastating and painful effect.
During June, Hitler
      was supervising the military plans
      to invade Poland.
General von Brauchitsch's top-secret
           army plan, was presented
      in Berchtesgaden
by June 15:
           The object of the operation
      is to destroy the Polish
           armed forces.
The political leadership demands
      that the war should begun
           by heavy surprise blows
      and lead to quick successes.
The intention of the Army High Command
           to prevent a regular mobilization
      of the Polish Army by surprise invasion. . .

22 June, General Keitel submitted
                    to Hitler
a 'preliminary timetable
                    for Case White'.
Hitler 'In main' agreed,
but 'so as not to disquiet the population
by calling up reserves on a larger scale
                    than usual . . .
civilian establishments, employers
                    or other private persons
who make inquiries should be told
                    men are being called up
for autumn maneuvers. . .'
                    'for reasons of security,
the cleaning of hospitals
                    in the frontier area
which the Supreme Command
                    of the Army proposed
should take place in the middle
                    of July must not be carried out.
The war was to be a total war
                    and required a total
mobilization of the resources
of the nation.
Hitler planned to draft seven million men.

Dr. Funk the minister of economics,
        duty was to arrange 'what work is
        to be given to prisoners of war
and to inmates of prisons
                    concentration camps
'greater use will be made
of the concentration camps wartime. . .'
'hundreds of thousands of workers
        from the Czech protectorate
are to be employed
        in supervision in Germany,
particularly in agriculture,
            and housed in hutments. . .'
Dr. Fink, the minister of interiors,
        assignment was to 'save labor in
        the public administration'
            which had increased
'from twenty to forty-fold---
            an impossible state of affairs.'
'In the transportation sphere
        Germany is at the moment
        not ready for war'
        a report from Colonel Rudolf Gercke,
    chief of the transportation Department
        of the Army General Staff. . .

The Germans had been smuggling
            into Danzig arms
            and Army officers

In civilian clothes
to train locals and for study tours.

4 August, polish diplomatic representatives
in Danzig informed the authorities
that Polish custom inspectors
had been given orders to carry out
their functions 'with arms'. . .
The Polish government would
'retaliate without delay
against the Free City.
If they attempted to obstruct
Polish officials.'

This enraged Hitler:
'would lead to an aggravation
of German-Polish relations. . .
for which the German government
must disclaim all responsibility.'

22 July, the Soviet press announced
in Moscow that Soviet-German
treaty negotiations like
had resumed in Berlin

23 July, France and England
awakened and agreed
to the Soviet proposal
for military staff talks

on how three nations might defend
themselves
against Hitler's armies.

2 June, the Soviets desired 'methods,
forms and extant' of military defense,
the others only could comprehend
a political agreement.

The governments of Budapest and Rome
expressed reservations:
24 July, Count Teleki, Premier of Hungary
in letters to Hitler and Mussolini:
'in event of a general conflict Hungary
will make her policy conform to the policy
of the axis.'. .
yet 'repeat that Hungary could not,
on moral grounds, be in a position
to take armed action against Poland.'

'NO POWER IN THE WORLD COULD PENETRATE
GERMANY'S WESTERN FORTIFICATIONS. NOBODY
IN ALL MY LIFE HAS BEEN ABLE TO FREIGHTEN ME,
AND THAT GOES FOR BRITAIN. NOR WILL I SURCUMB
TO THE OFT PERDICTED NERVOUS
BREAKDOWN. . .THE SOVIET GOVERNMENT
WOULD NOT FIGHT AGAINST US. . . THEY WOULD,
HOWEVER, TRY TO ENRICH THEMSELVES. (HITLER)

'Well, Ribbentrop, what do you want?' said Ciano,
The Corridor or Danzig?'
'Not that anymore, we want war!'
declared Ribbentrop.
Ciano's position that a Polish conflict could not be
localized was dismissed.
He moved on to Obersalzberg, where Hitler
cordially greeted him.

'I personally am absolutely convinced that
the western democracies will,
in the last resort, recoil unloading
a general war.'
The Italian Foreign Minister stated
'that he hoped the Fuehrer would prove right
but did not believe it.'
'I returned to Rome, completely disgusted
with the Germans, with their leaders,
with their way of doing things. . .
They have betrayed us and lied to us.
Now they will be dragging us into an adventure
which we have not wanted
and which might compromise
the regime and the country as a whole.'
(from the diary of Count Galeazzo Ciano)

PAIN

I began work on PART TWO of present poem,
    the first week I desired to return to work,
nor could I continue without income.
        I first began half days
    the next month. After a week
    the Mind Control drugs were increased.
I became painfully restless, and pacing.
        Laying in bed the only relief.
Not able to think the pain would end,
    in six months, as in the past.
        Bed became my only desire.
    I could not at first listen to music,
            but after a month or two
this became my bed addiction,
        then my return to life.
One Saturday I purchased a CD changer,
        I was up all day,
    and began to walk to Mall on weekends.

THE NAZI-SOVIET NON-AGGRESSION TREATY.

14 August, the German ambassador contacted
        Molotov and read to him 'verbatim'
            German-Russian relations
        wrote Ribbentrop,
    had 'come to a historic turning point.

There exist no real conflict of interest
    between Germany and Russia. . .
It had gone well with both countries
    when they were friends
and badly when they were enemies.'

The Military Conference.

The great drama is now approaching its climax.'
Britain 'has no leaders of real caliber.

The men I got know at Munich
    are not the kind that start a new world war'
                            (Hitler)

Operation Himmler
                'canned goods'
'Canaris checked with section 1,
        Himmler Heydrick,
        Obersalzberg:
    150 Polish uniforms with accessories
        for upper Silesia.'
    (General Halder's diary.)
On of the S.D., Heydrich, personally
ordered me to stimulate an attack
        on radio station near Gleiwitz
    near the Polish boarder and to make
        it appear that the attacking forces
            consisted of Poles,

Heydrich said:
'Practical proof is needed for these
attacks of the Poles for foreign press
as well as German propaganda.'
My instructions were to seize
the radio station and hold it
long enough to permit Polish
speaking Germans who would
be put at my disposal to broadcast
a speech in Polish. . . In which
it would appear that Polish soldiers
were attacking German troops. . .
12 or 13 Condemned criminals
who dressed in Polish uniforms
and left dead on the ground of the scene
of the Incident to show that they
have been killed while attacking.'
(Alfred Naujocks at Nuremberg)

That until recently the Soviet Government
had proceeded on the assumption
that the Government are seeking
occasion for clashes with the Soviet Union
. . . Not to mention the fact that
the German Government by means
of the so-called Anti-Comintern Pact,
were endeavoring to create,

and have created, the united frontier
that have excited,
of a number of States
against the Soviet Union.
If, however, the German Government
now undertakes a change
from the old policy in the direction
of a serious improvement
in political relations
with the Soviet Union,
the Soviet Government
can only welcome such a change,
and are, for their part, prepared
to revise their policy
in the sense of a serious improvement
with respect to Germany. . . (Molotov)
August 1942, Stalin related to Churchill
his reasoning:
'We formed the impression
that the British and French
Governments were not resolved
to go to war if Poland were attacked,
but that they hoped the diplomatic
line-up of Britain, French, and Russia
would deter Hitler
We were sure it would not. . .
'How many divisions, will France
send against Germany on mobilization?'
'About a hundred.'

How many will England? 'Two and Two,
more later.' 'Ah, two and two
more later,' 'Do you know, how many
divisions we will have to put
in the Russian front if we go to war
with Germany?'
'More than three hundred.'

Apparently the announcement
of a German-Soviet Agreement
is taken in some quarters in Berlin
to indicate that intervention
by Great Britain on behalf of Poland
is no longer a contingency
that need be reckoned with.
No greater mistake could be made.
Whatever may prove to be the nature
of the German-Soviet Agreement,
it cannot alter Great Britain's
obligation to Poland. . .
(Chamberlain in a letter to Hitler.)

'. . . on the basis of proposal
of truly unparalleled magnanimity. . .
to loosen a wave appalling terrorism
against the one and a half million
German inhabitants living
in Poland. . .atrocities. . .are terrible

for victims but intolerable for a Great Power
                such as the German Reich. . .
          that it can make no change
in the determination of the Reich Government
          to safeguard the interest of the Reich. . .
                Germany, if attached by England,
          will be found prepared and determined.'
                (Hitler's response to Chamberlain.)

22 August, 1939; Military Conference.
          'I have called you together
to give you a picture of the political situation
          in order that you may have some insight
                into individual factors on which
          I have based my irrevocable decision
to act and In order to strengthen your
                confidence. After that we shall
          discuss military details.'
'My own personality and that of Mussolini.
                Essentially all depends on me,
                on my existence, because
of my political talents. Furthermore
                that fact that probably
          no one will again have the confidence
of the whole German people as I have.
                There will probably never again
                in the future be a man
          with more authority than I have.
          My existence is therefore a factor

of great value. But I can be eliminated
by a criminal or a lunatic'
The enemy had another hope,
that Russia would become our enemy
after the conquest of Poland.
The enemy did not count on
my great power of resolution.
Our enemy are little worms.
I saw them In Munich. . .
'The most iron determination on our part.
No shrinking back from anything.
Everyone must hold the view that
we have been determined
to fight the Western powers
right from the start. . .
A life-death struggle. . .
A long period of peace
would not do us any good. . .
A manly bearing. . .we have better men. . .
The destruction of Poland has priority. . .
Close your hearts to pity! And brutality!
Eighty million people must obtain
what is right. . .The stronger man is right. . .
Be harsh and remorseless!
Be steeled against all signs of compassion!
Whoever has pondered over this
world order knowns its meaning lies
In the success of the best by means of force...'

If Germany attacks Poland and the latter's allies
    open a counterattack against Germany. . .
in view of the present state of Italian War
      preparations. . . Our intervention can,
  nevertheless, take place at once
    if Germany delivers to us
the immediately the military supplies
    and raw materials to resist
the attack. . . At our meetings the war
    envisaged for 1942. . .
        (Mussolini to Hitler)

On the day that England gave
  her official guarantee to Poland
the Fuehrer called me on the telephone
    and told me that he had stopped
the planned invasion of Poland.
  I asked him whether
this was just temporary
  or for good.
He said, No I will have to see whether
  we can eliminate
    British intervention.
(Goering at Nuremberg)

'COMPLETE CHAOS IN POLAND---
GERMAN FAMILIES FLEE---
POLISH SOLDIERS TO EDGE OF GERMAN BOADER!'
'THIS PLAYING WITH FIRE GOING TOO FAR---
THREE GERMAN PASSENGER PLANES SHOT
AT BY POLES---IN THE CORRIDOR MANY GERMAN
FARMHOUSES IN FLAMES!' 'THE WHOLE OF POLAND
IN WAR FEVER! 1,500,000 MEN MOBLIALIZED!'
UNINTERUPRUPTED TROOP TRANSPORT TOWARD
THE FRONTIER! CHAOS IN UPPER SILESIA!'

'What implements of war and raw materials
        you require and with what time?'
'That all material must be in Italy before
            the beginning of hostilities.'

'IMPOSSIBLE!' (Hitler)
'If the blood of France and Germany
        flows again as it did twenty-five years
in a longer and even more murderous war,
each of the two people will fight confidence
            in its victory, but the most certain
            victors will be the forces of destruction
        and barbarism.'   (DALADIER)

'Get everything ready for morning Mobilization Day.

     Attack starts, 1 September.
Plan: We demand Danzig, Corridor through Corridor,
     and plebiscite on the same basis as Saar. . .
       England will perhaps accept. . .
     Poland probably not. . .Wedge between them.'
'If there should be war, then I shall build U-boats,
build U-boats, U-boats, U-boats, U-boats, . . . ---
I shall build airplanes, build airplanes, airplanes,
airplanes, and I shall annihilate my enemies. . .'
build U-boats, U-boats, build airplanes, airplanes.

'At the time I was in touch with Halifax
by special courier (Dahlerus) outside
the regular diplomatic channels.' (Goering)

'Herr Dahlerus, you know England so well,
     can you give me any reason for my
     perpetual failure to come to an agreement'

     'lack of confidence'
Idiots! Have I ever told a lie in my life?
        (Hitler)

'As we work to solve our economic problems,
let us tap the well of human spirit.'
     (Reagan: AFL-CIO Convention, March 30, 1981)

Statement by Assistant to the President
David R. Gergen. About the Attempted
Assassination of the President, March, 30, 1981.

'Good Afternoon. This is to confirm the statements
made at George Washington Hospital that
the President was shot once in the left side,
this afternoon, as he left the hotel. His condition
is stable. A decision is now being made whether
or not to remove the bullet. The White House and
the Vice President are in communication, and
the Vice President is now en route to Washington. He
is expected to arrive in the city this afternoon.
Mrs. Reagan is currently with the President
at the Hospital. . .'

The German Government accordingly agree accept
the British Government's offer
of their good offices in securing the dispatch
to Berlin of a Polish emissary
with full powers. They count on the arrival
of this emissary on Wednesday.

30 August, 1939.
The German Government will immediately
draw up proposals for solution
acceptable to themselves and will,

If possible, place these at the disposal
    of the British Government
    before the arrival of Polish negotiator.

Midnight 20 June, 1791, disguised as a manservant
    Louis VXI left the Tuileries
        with his family, and arrived at Varennes
        the night of 21 of June.
He was recognized and barricades
        were erected on the bridge
            across the River Aire.
An unruly mob gathered, and the King
        head toward Paris, guarded by
            the National guardsman.
He planned to join Bouille's army,
        and on to the Austrian army
            in the Netherlands,
        the return to Paris, dissolve
the Assembly and clubs, and return to
        absolute power.
    He had earlier begun
secret negotiations with other monarchs.
        The King had certain aim,
the re-establishment of absolute power.

02 February, 1988;
Reagan's position is deteriorating
           more and more every day.
It has become apparent that as regards
           South Africa, and his obsession
     with the 'contras', his anti-communist
           nature has destroyed
     his administration.
We are only lucky it is his last year.
This man is brainwashed,
                crime after crime,
     is wiped away. Public pressure
           has no effect on the man.
The space program failed,
His MX-missiles are questionable,
     because Capitalism Is greed,
           a Judas to itself, first money.
The capitalist press admits 10,000 homeless
                in Philadelphia.
The capitalist system sends its dropouts
           to prisons, asylums, slums,
     and now that slums have become
                an investment, the streets.
The society is not only the rich,
           but one of 'The American Dream'.
The capitalist proletariat is recycled
           generation after generation
via the capitalist-controlled press, and media.
     The degradation of the Savings and Loan

institutions have created an avenue
for corruption unprecedented
in democratic society.
The working class will pay dearly
for its election of capitalist
'hand-picked' movie star.
An epidemic, AIDS, has infected
the 'pleasure' worship of the
decadent age, of Carterism,
and the mammon of Reaganism.
Drug-running is denounced,
yet a way to finance their
Imperialistic mercenaries.

The Russian revolution was cruelly defeated in 1906;
The Russian Bolsheviks were defeated in July 1917;
over 15,000 German communists were killed
as a result of wily provocation and cunning
maneuvers of Scheidemann and Noske
working hand and glove with the bourgeoise
and monarchist generals;
White terror is ragging in Finland and Hungary.
But in all cases and in all countries Communism
is becoming steeled
its roots are deep that persecution
does not weaken it, does not debilitate it,
but strengthen it. Only one thing is lacking
to enable us to march forward

more confidently and firmly to victory,
        namely, the universal and thoroughly
    and thought-out appreciation by all Communist
            In all countries of the necessity
of displaying the utmost, in their tactics.
                    (LENIN)

SUPREME COMMANDER OF THE ARMED FORCES
MOST SECRET

Berlin, 31 August 1939
Directive No. 1 for Conduct of War.
Now that all the political possibilities
    of disposing by peaceful means
        of a situation on the eastern Frontier
    which is intolerable for Germany
                    are exhausted.
        I have determined on a solution by force.

2. . . . .The attack of Poland is to be carried out
            in accordance with the preparations
    made for Case White, with the alterations
    which result, where the Army is concerned,
Allotment of tasks and the operational target
                remain unchanged.
Date of attack: 1 September 1939
This timing also applies to the operation ay Gdynia,
    Bay of Danzig and the Dirschau Bridge.

3. ... On land, the German Western Frontier
    is not to be crossed without expressed
permission.
    At sea, the same applies for all warlike actions
      or actions which could be regarded
         as such.
4. ... If Britain and France open hostilities
      against Germany, it is the task of
      the Wehrmacht formations operating
        in the west to observe their forces
    as much as possible and thus maintain
        the conditions for a victorious
      conclusion of the operations
        against Poland.
    Within these limits enemy forces
        and their military-economic
    resources are to be damaged as much
        as possible.
    Orders to go over to the attack I reserve,
        in any case, for myself. . .
    In Luftwaffe in disturbing British supplies
        by sea, the armaments industry,
        and the transport
        of troops to France.

    'I replied, I was asked for an interview
      as ambassador, to present a
        declaration from my Government.'

'The Polish Government are favorably
considering the British Government suggestions,
and will them a formal reply on the subject
during the next few hours.'   (Lipski)

THE VICTOR WILL NOT ASK AFTERWARD
WHETHER HE TOLD THE TRUTH OR NOT
IN STARTING OR WAGING A WAR IT IS NOT
RIGHT THAT MATTERS, BUT VICTORY.
                    (HITLER)
WE SECURED PEACE FOR OUR COUNTRY
FOR ONE AND A HALF YEARS, AS WELL AS
AN OPPORTUNITY OF PREPARING OUR FORCES
FOR DEFENSE IF FASCIST GERMANY RISKED
ATTACKING OUR COUNTRY IN DEFIANCE OF THE
PACT. THIS WAS A DEFINATE GAIN FOR OUR
COUNTRY AND A LOSS FOR FASCIST GERMANY.
                    (STALIN)

17 July 1791; the Cordeliers met on
            the Champ-de-Mars to sign
    republican petition on the altar of France.
        On the pretext that the crowd was
    disorderly and a danger to public order,
        the Assembly ordered the Mayor
    of Paris to disperse the demonstrators,
            martial law was proclaimed.

The National Guard fired on
the unarmed crowd,
killing some, fifty dead.
A terror spread, arrest were numerous,
several democratic papers were ceased,
the Cordelier's Club closed.
Robespierre inspired the Democratic group,
while La Fayette and Lameth
joined forces in the Feuillants, ready
to negotiate with the King and Royalist.

THE WILL TO POWER AS ART

Our religion, morality, and philosophy
are decadence forms of man,
countermovement art.
The artist-philosopher. Higher concept
of art. Whether a man can place
himself so far distant from
other men that he can form them?
(Preliminary exercises:
1. he who forms himself, the hermit.
2. the artist hitherto, as a perfecter
on a small scale, working on material.)
Apollonian-Dionysian --- There are two
conditions In which art appears in
like a force of nature and disposes
of whether he will or not

the compulsion to have visions
and as a compulsion to an orgiastic state.
       Both conditions are rehearsed
              in ordinary life, too, but weaker:
       in dream and intoxication. But the same
antithesis obtains between dream and in
              intoxication:
 both release artistic powers in us,
       but different ones: the dream those
or vision, association, poetry; intoxication
       those of gesture, passion, song, dance.
In Dionysian intoxication there is sensuality
       and voluptuousness: they are not lacking
in the Apollonian. There must also be
              a difference in tempo in the two
conditions --- The extreme calm In certain
              sensations of intoxication
(more strictly: the retardation of feelings
       of time and space) lies to be reflected
In vision of the calmest gestures and types
              of soul. The classical style is
essentially a representation of the calm,
simplification, abbreviation, concentration---
              the highest feeling power is
       concentrated in the classical type.
To react slowly; a great consciousness,
              no feeling or struggle.
Artist, if they are good, are (physically as well)

strong, full of surplus energy, powerful
animals, sensual; without
a certain overheating of the sensual
system a Raphael is unthinkable---
Making music is another way of making
Children, chastity is merely the economy
of an artist---and in any event,
even with artistic fruitfulness ceases
when potency ceases---Artist should see
nothing as it is, but fuller, simpler,
stronger: to that end, their lives must
contain a kind of youth and spring,
a kind of habitual intoxication.
(NIETZCHE)

NATI(ONALSOZIALSTISCHE DEUTSCHE
ARBEITERPARTEI)

'We must ally ourselves the powerful
institutions of the State, in order
to take the power and subvert
a revolutionary movement,
the Socialists principles will become
our front.'
'We must eliminate our opponents, and
seize complete power, Chancellor
is not complete.'
'The Socialist Democratic Party repels me.

I witnessed a mass demonstration
of Viennese workers. In oppressed anxiety
        I finally left the place and sauntered
homeward. At home I began to study
the Social Democratic text, its organization,
        reflect on its psychology and
                political techniques: They knew
        the art of propaganda, they could create
a spiritual terror which this movement everts,
particularly, on the bourgeois, which neither
        morally mentally equal to such attacks,
        at a given sign it unleashes
        a veritable barrage or lies and slanders
                against whatever adversary seams
        most dangerous, until the nerves
of the attacked person breakdown . . .
This is the tactic based on precise
        calculation of all human weaknesses,
        and its result will lead to success with
almost mathematical certainty. . .I achieved
                an equal understanding
of the importance of physical terror
                toward the individual and the masses.
For while in the ranks of their supporters
                the victory achieved seems
        a triumph of the justice of their own cause,
the defeated adversary in most cases despairs
        of the success of any further resistance '
                (HITLER)

1 September 1939; German troops
 moved in haste across the Polish broader.

ALL MEN SHALL HATE EACH OTHER

THE END OF PART TWO

PART THREE

June 12, 1986, I arrived in Praha (Prague)
for my second visit.
For four years I have not been permitted
to travel by the State government.
The last time I have been in Europe
was 1979, now spending six days in Praha.
Having been robbed on a train from Wien,
to Warsaw, I had little money. This was the first
time I had taken a sleeping car,
resting naturally after such a troublesome
summer. Earlier having received
some money from the sale of my home.
Careless only this one time, I paid dearly.

Having money only from vouchers,
was very disheartening.
It was seven years in waiting, I had twice
planned to leave once having
plane ticket, but twice this action was aborted.
'Hello, I am in Brno, everything is fine.
The food is good, great! How's everything?
'Where are you so we may look on the map?'
'I am in Brno; it is in the south-central
part of the country.'

The first principle of the Democratic Party
            is that it is a front organization
of the decadent Capitalist, and religious
groups. The name suggests a government
            of the people, yet in reality it
is an organization which is financed and
controlled by the Capitalist, not the people.

The appearance of submission
                to the forces that control society
becomes necessary to avoid
                    imprisonment.
Thousands waste in prisons who have resisted
            the submission of capitalist society.
    I have seen this myself.

Let us now picture ourselves by way of change,
        a community of free individuals,
            carrying out their work with
the means of production in common,
        which labor-power of all the different
            individuals is continuously applied
as the combined labor-power
            of the community. Everything produced
by him was exclusively the result
        of his own personal labor,
and theretofore simply an object
            of use for himself.

The total product of our community
is a social product. One portion
serves as fresh means of production and remains
social. But another portion
is consumed by the members as means
of subsistence. A distribution
of this portion amongst them
is consequently necessary. The mode of this
distribution will vary with
the productive organization of the community,
and the degree of historical development
attained by producers.
We will assume, but merely for the sake of a parallel
production of commodities, that the share
of each individual producer
in the means of subsistence is determined
by his labor---time would,
in that case, play a double part.
Its apportionment In accordance with a definite
plan maintains the proper proportion
the different kinds of work to be done
and the various wants of the communit.
On the other hand, it also serves as a measure
of the portion of the common labor
borne by each individual consumption.
(MARX)

We left Praha, our first stop was Lidice.
The museum there was still under
construction. We entered a portion,
but will speak of this village in our studies.
I did much less, than Jan Kubis
and Josef Gabeik,
yet were not my actions just?
Must we not criticize and awaken injustice?
We then traveled through beautiful countryside,
past a few golf courses, till we arrived
in Karlovy Vary, in western Bohemia.
What an excellent city,
one of the most pleasant
I have ever set foot in.
One of the older romantic colonnaded Spas
was under reconstruction,
but it will never rival the modern Spa.
The water shoots out of the ground,
and it is delightful to stroll the walks
of the little Tepia river,
lined with quaint shops, and occasionally
encounter someone with a little cup
of spring water.
The one shop where I purchased stamps,
the gentleman was quite kind,
he was very conciliatory, yet allowed
me to make my own decision.
The very important purchase,

since I am sending postcards.
It contrasts the experiences
I have had in a few government
Post Offices in South Jersey.

At noon 25 July, 1934, 154 members of the SS
Standarte 89, dressed in Austrian Army
uniforms, stormed into the Federal Chancellery
and shot Dollfuss in the throat
at range of two feet.
A few blocks away Nazis seized the radio station
and broadcast the news that
Dollfuss had resigned.
Hitler was witnessing 'Das Rheingold'
at annual Wagner Festival In Bayreuth,
Freidelind Wagner who was near Hitler states:
'After the performance the Fuehrer
was most excited.
This excitement mounted as he told
us the horrible news. . .
ordered dinner in the restaurant
as usual.
'I must go across for an hour and show myself,
or people will think I had something
to do with this.'
Prior to July 1934 the Austrian Nazis,
with weapons and dynamite
furnished by Germany, has instituted

a reign of terror, blowing up railways,
power stations and government buildings
and murdering supporters
of the Dollfuss clerical-fascist government.
Government forces, led by Dr. Kurt Schuschnigg,
quickly regained control, and the rebels,
were arrested and thirteen
of them hanged.

Mussolini mobilized four divisions
on the Brenner Pass.

In a series of interviews, Hitler,
'War will not come again' 'a more profound
impression than any other of the evil
of war causes' 'Germany's
problems cannot be settled by war'
Hitler's rearmament plan did not cease,
They intensified.
The army was ordered
from 100,000 to 300,000
by 1 October 1934.
Fuehrer's instructions: No mention
must be made of a displacement
of 25-26 tons, but only improved
10,000 tons ships. . .
The Fuehrer demands complete secrecy
on the construction of U-boats.
On 16 March, Sunday ---

The Chancellor decreed
a law establishing universal military service
and a peace time army
of a half-million men.

On 21 May, he delivered a speech
to the Reichstag:
'The blood shed on European continent
the last three hundred years
bears no proportion to the national
result of the events.
In the end France has remained France,
Germany Germany, Poland Poland,
and Italy Italy.
What dynastic egotism, political passion,
and patriotic kindness have
attained in the way of apparently
far-reaching political changes by shedding
rivers of blood have, as regards
national feelings, done no more than
touched the skin of the nations.
It has not substantially altered their
fundamental characters.

If these states had applied a fraction
of their sacrifices to wiser purposes
the success would certainly
have been greater and more permanent. . .
the subjection and domination

of an alien people as a proceeding which
sooner or later changes and weakens
the Victor internally, and
and eventually brings about his defeat. . .
No! National Socialism wants
peace because of its fundamental
Convictions. . . Germany needs
peace and desires peace . . .'
Germany neither intents nor wishes
to interfere in the internal affairs
of Austria, to annex Austria,
or to conclude an Anschluss.
The German government is ready
to agree to any limitations which
leads to the abolition
of the heaviest arms. . . heaviest tanks. . .
Whoever light the torch of war in Europe
can wish for nothing but chaos.
We, however, live in the firm conviction
that our time will be fulfilled
not the decline but the renaissance
of the West. . .
That Germany may make an imperishable
contribution to the great work
in our proud hope and our
unshakable belief. . .'

The Times of London:
The speech turns out to be reasonable,
straightforward and comprehensive.
No one reads it with an impartial mind
can doubt that the point of policy laid down
by Herr Hitler may fairly constitute the basis
of a complete settlement with Germany---
a free equal and strong Germany instead of
the prostrate Germany upon peace was imposed
         sixteen years ago.

1 October 1935, Mussolini's armies invaded
Abyssinia, in defiance of the Covenant of League
of Nations.

1 March 1935, Hitler defied his generals
ordering the small German forces to occupy
the Rhineland. 'Germany no longer feels bound
by the Locarno Treaty. In the interest of the
primitive rights of the people to the security
of their frontier and safeguarding at their
defense, the German government has
re-establish as of today, the absolute and
unrestricted sovereignty of the Reich in
the demilitarized zone'   (Hitler)

'What would have happened, if anybody
other than myself had been at the head of

Reich! Anyone you care to mention would
have lost nerve. I was obliged to lie, and
who saved us was my unshakable obstinacy
and my amazing aplomb'.   (Hitler)

1 May, 1936, Italian forces entered Addis
   Ababa, the Abyssinian capital.

16 July 1936, France leads a military revolt
In Spain and a civil war broke loose.

'The battle we are approaching demands
              a colossal measure of production
       capacity. No limit on rearmament can
              be visualized. The only alternative
              are victory or destruction.
We live in the time when the final battle
              is in sight. We are already on that
              threshold of mobilization
                   and we are already at war.
All that is lacking is the actual shooting.'
       (Goering in secret to a group
                   of industrialist.)

Mussolini accepted Hitler's invitation
       to visit Germany.
       26 September 1937'
outfitted in a new uniform
       he crossed the Alps into

the Third Reich.
Hitler wished to impress him with Germany's
strength; Parades of SS and the troops,
to army maneuvers in Mecklenburg,
to the armament factories in Ruhr.
A gigantic crowd of one million people
to hear the two leaders, speak.
He returned to Italy convinced that
the ultimate victory is with Hitler.

I. War on two fronts with main struggle
on the West.
STRATEGIC CONCENTRATION 'ROT'
II. War on two fronts with the main struggle
in southwest.
STRATEGIC CONCENTRATION 'GREUN'
The war in the East can begin with a surprise
German operation against Czechoslovakia
in order to party the imminent attack
of a superior enemy coalition.
The necessary condition to justify such
an action politically and in eyes
of international law must be beforehand.
I.   Armed intervention against Austria.
(Special case 'Otto')
II.   Warlike complications with Red Spain.
(Special case 'Richard')
Iii. England, Poland, Lithuania take part in war
against us.   (Rot/Gruen)

The object of the operation-armed
intervention in Austria in the Monarchy-will
                compel Austria by armed forced
                        to give up restoration.
Making use of the domestic political dissention
                of Austrian people, there will a march
to this end in the general direction of Vienna,
                and any resistance will be broken.
The history of all ages---the Roman Empire
                and the British Empire---had proved
        that expansion could only be carried out
by breaking down resistance and taking risks,
setbacks were inevitable. There had never. . .
                been spaces without a master, and
        there were none today, the attacker
                always comes up against a possessor.
Germany's problem could be solved only by
                means of force, and this was never
without attendant risk. . .Our first objective. . .
                must be to overthrow
Czechoslovakia and Austria simultaneously
        in order to remove the threat to our flank
        in a possible operation against the West.
                                (Hitler)

Foreign Minister Baron von Neurath:
        'I was extremely upset at Hitler's speech,
Because it knocked the bottle out of the whole
                        foreign policy

which I consistently pursued.'
General von Fritsch visited Hitler
on 9 November. . .
On that occasion I tried to show him
that his policy would lead to world war,
and that I would have no part in it. . .
I called his attention to the danger of war
and to the serious warning
of the generals. . . When despite all
arguments he held to his opinion.
I told him that he would have to
find another Foreign Minister.
(Neurath)
'crowded into Goering's anteroom
In hope getting orders when I was still
trying to get a voice of reason heard.'

'FROM NOW ON I TAKE OVER PERSONALLY
THE COMMAND OF THE WHOLE ARMED FORCES'
'HITLER'
'What influence a woman, even without realizing
it, can exert on the history
of a country and thereby on the world'
Colonel Alfred Jodl's diary

26 January 1938
'One has the feeling of living in a fateful hour
of the German people.'
'The General Field Marshall in a high state

Excitement. Reason not known.
Apparently a personal matter.
He retired for eight days
to an unknown place. (Jodl)
Chief of the General Staff, General Beck,
to Keitel: One cannot tolerate the highest
ranking soldier marrying a whore.'
Colonel General Freiherr Warner von Fritsch,
The Commander in Chief of the Army,
Was revealed been guilty of homosexual
offenses under Section 175
of German Criminals Code.
'A lot of stinking lies!' (von Fritsch)

'We did not gather here to speak
of the weather.'
(Adolf Hitler to Kurt von Schuschnigg,
Chancellor Austria.)
You have done everything to avoid
a friendly policy. . .The whole history
of Austria is just one uninterrupted
act of high treason.
That was so in the past
and is no better today.
This historical paradox must now
reach its long-overdue and. . .
And I can tell you right now.
Herr Schuschnigg, that I am absolutely
determined to make an end

of all this. The German Reich is one
of great powers, and nobody
will raise his voice if it settles
its border problems.

13 February. In the afternoon General Keitel
asks Admiral Canaris and myself
(General Jodl) to come to his apartment.
He tells us that the Fuehrer's order is that
Military pressure by shamming military
action should be kept a until the 15th.
Proposals for these measures are drafted
and submitted to the Fuehrer
by telephone for approval.
14 February. The effect is quick and strong.
In Austria the impression
Is created that Germany
Is undertaking
serious military preparations.

The Declaration of Pillnitz (27 August 1791)

The flight of the King and his arrest
aroused great deal of emotion
throughout Europe.
'What a frightful example
that presents to us all.'
(The Mind of Prussia)

The Emperor Leopold proposed
        that the Courts of Europe cooperate
to save the French crown,
                and the Royal Family.
The emigres were now joined
        by the Comte de Provence,
published a manifesto announcing
the imminent invasion of France,
        attacked the assembly,
and organized troops under
        the Prince de Conde,
on the Elector of Treves's territory of Coblenz.

'The most dangerous class of all consists
        of the large number of people
who have lost as the result of the Revolution,
        and more particularly
                of the many great landowners
rich merchants and men who because
        of their arrogance and vast wealth
can not tolerate the principles of equality
                but regret of the nobility
to which they themselves aspired.
Men who, in the analysis,
        loathe the new constitution
which is the very mother of equality.'
                (ISNARD)

'. . . even though the result seems excessively bad,
    we shall be able to turn all this
    to our advantage much sooner
    than anyone could imagine.'
    (Maria—Antoinette on 16 November elections)

'In place of civil war
        there be a political war
                in Europe and this change
        would greatly improve the situation.
The physical and moral conditions of France
        Is such as to make it impossible
for her to resist even a partial campaign.
                (LOUIS XVI)
'The fools! They do not see that
it is in our interest!' (Marie-Antoinette)

'. . .Let us mark out in advance a place for
traitors, and let that place be the scaffold!'
                (Gaudet)

'. . . A people that had just won its liberty
        after ten centuries of slavery. . .
    needs a war in order to bring about
        consolidation, '   (Brissot)
'. . . The moment has therefore arrived
        at last, when France
must be seen in the eyes of all Europe
    to be a free nation which is prepared

to defend and maintain the liberty
   that has been won.'   (Brissot)
'. . . War at such a time as this is a blessing
         to a nation, and the only calamity
      that we should fear is that
         there will not be war. . . It is
      the national interest alone
         that councils us to declare war.'
                  (Brissot)
'War! War! That is the cry that is being heard
         In every corner of the Empire,
. . . The cry that is now ringing to our ears!'
'The moment has come for a new crusade,
         a crusade for liberty the world over.'
                  (Brissot)
'. . . a war by the people of Europe
            against their Kings.' (Isnard)
Robespierre stood almost alone
      in his opposition to the war policy
of the Brissotins. In a speech In January 1792,
         he pointed out that war would
      please the Court, the emigres,
            and supporters of La Fayette.
'Is it not here In Paris? . . . is there, then
      no link between Coblenz
   and another place which is not far from
   where we are meeting at this moment?'
Start by taking a long look at your internal
   position here in France; put your house in order

before you try it elsewhere.'
The revolution must first purge the army,
take control of the Court, and deal
with its enemies that remain in France,
before it could dissipate the ruling class
of Europe. Robespierre also foresaw
the possibility that a general might put
personal ambition and interest above liberty.
No! I have no confidence whatever
In the generals and, with one or two
honorable exceptions, I should say that
almost all of them regret
the passing of the old order of things
and the favors that were freely
distributed by the Court.
I base my case only on the people,
On the people and them alone.
(Robespierre)

Large concentrations of troops
are advancing on our frontiers,
and all those who regard liberty
with horror are taking up arms
to destroy our constitution.
Citizens! La Patria est en danger.
(Brissot; 11 July)

If there are men who want to build
a Republic on the ruins
of the present Constitution,
then the full severity of the law
must be used again at them
in same way as it is involved against
the partisans of the second chamber
and the counter-revolutionaries
at Coblenz.   (Brissot; 26 July)

The rising against the monarchy
of 10 August 1792
was a demonstration
at the Federation of the representatives
of the people of France,
and not just the citizens of Paris.
Forty-seven of the forty-eight
sections voted to abridge
the King of his Crown.
'Citizens, have you come here to take part
in a purely empty ceremonial,
that of renewing the Federation
of 14 July? (Robespierre)
. . . concerted scheming of the Court
and certain intriguing elements
within the Legislative. . .'
(Robespierre)

The Brunswick Manifesto

Marie-Antoinette had asked the monarchs
allied to France, to write a declaration
that threatened with the penalty
of death those national guardsmen
and civilians who dared to
'to defend themselves against
the invading armies, or commit
the 'slightest outrage' against
the royal family, with
'vengeance that shall be exemplary
and unforgettable, with the town
of Paris handed over to the full rigors
of military justice and complete
overthrow of the existing authorities.'

La Commune insurrectionnelle
The suburbs rose and marched on the Tuileries
with the federers from the provinces,
and at the Tuileries the National Guard
to the side of the insurgents.
At eight o'clock the first to appear
the men of Marseille. They were
allowed to enter
the Palace grounds, but the Swiss Guards
opened fire and drove them back.
But once the representatives
of the Paris suburbs arrived

and offered their help, the Federer's
resumed their attack and made
to storm the Tuileries. Around
ten o'clock, on the orders
of the King, the besieges troops
stopped firing on the crowd.
(Albert Goboul)

THE OVERTHROW OF THE MONARCHY

When the outcome of the fighting
was certain, the Assembly declared
the King was suspended of his duties.
They voted that the Convention
be elected by universal suffrage.

THE PASSIVE CITIZENS URGED ON
BY ROBESPIERRE
EMBRACED REVOLUTIONARY POLITICS.
No single class of citizens alone
has the right to grant
itself the exclusive privileges
of saving the country.
23 May 1988. I arrived
for my third visit to Praha.
Much had changed, and of course
the city was even more beautiful
than before.

The Czechoslovak Republic,
     was the most liberal
  of the countries I have visited.
The view the Capitalist Media and
     and the United States
  government is contrary.
Shortly before I arrived a great moment
     had taken in the history
of Socialism. The Nicaraguan government
     finally crushed Reagan by
  meeting his propagandistic demands.
With the summit meeting to take place,
     and the above occurrence:
  a calm, a great hope of democracy,
     and the further 'liberation',
  now in the mind of the people.
The end of the 'economic blockade'
     is also a desired reality.
Arriving in Praha I went to
     the Reiseboro of DDR
  on Parizska street it took one day
     to reserve hotels
  the cities I planned to visit were:
Dresden, Berlin (Potsdam), Leipzig, Erfurt,
(Weimar), Karl-Marx Stadt, and
     return to Praha (Prague),
       for two nights.
Let me describe the city of Prague for you:
     because of an electrical storm,

we left JFK airport in New York
five and a half hours late.
The airport is divided into two sections
one on each side of highway.
Its passenger sections
is an early-modern building.
At first you are deceived
and do not notice
the modern sculpture in the walls.
I went through customs quickly
my bags arrived shortly
they were not opened or searched.
The one guard was same person
as two years ago.
I was not required to exchange any money.
I had two vouchers for half board.
Though I needed money
in order to get to the hotel
Panorama, where I was staying
for the first three nights.
*****Praha and DDR in part four continued*****

Over ten million live in two of the states
Adjoining our frontiers. . .
There must be no doubt about one thing.
Political separation from the Reich
May not lead to deprivation
Of rights---that is, the general rights

Of self-determination. It is unbearable
For a world power to know there
Are racial comrades at its side who
Are constantly being afflicted
With the severest suffering for their
Sympathy or unity with the whole Nation,
Its destiny and its Weltanschauung.
To the interests of the German Reich
Belong the protection of those things
German peoples who are not in a position
To secure along our frontiers
Their political and spiritual freedom
By their own efforts.
20 February speech set off massive
Nazis demonstrations in Austria.
24 February broadcast Schuschnigg reply:
'Red—' 'White' 'Red—', until were dead.'
Twenty thousand Nazis in Graz wrecked
The loudspeakers and destroyed
The Austrian flag, waved swastika banners.
Seyes-Inquart had personal command
Of the police, who were ordered
To do nothing.
The German government today handed
To President Miklas an ultimatum,
With a time, limit, ordering him
To nominate as Chancellor a person
Designated by the German government. . .
Otherwise, German troops would

Invade Austria.
I declare before the world that the reports
Launched in Germany concerning
Disorders by the workers,
the shedding of streams of blood
And the creation of a situation
Beyond the control of the Austrian
Government are lies from A to Z.
President Miklas has asked me to tell
The people of Austria
That we have yielded to forces
Since we are not prepared even
In this terrible hour to shed blood.
We have decided to order the troops
To offer no resistance.
So, I take leave of the Austrian people
With a German word of farewell,
Uttered from the depth of my heart.
God protect Austria.
(Schuschnigg)

HIS MAJESTY'S GOVERNMENT FEELS
BOUND TO REGISTER A PROTEST
IN THE STRONGEST TERMS.'
(Chamberlain)

I WAS COMPLETELY ABANDONED AT HOME
AND ABROAD.   (President Miklas)

In Linz, Hitler: : :
When years ago, I went forth from thus town
        I bore within me precisely
            The same profession of faith which today
                Fills my heart. Judge the depths
            Of my emotion when after so many years
I have been able to bring that profession
            Of faith to its fulfillment.
        If providence once called me forth to
            This town to be leader of the Reich,
        It must be in so doing have charged me
                With a mission, and that mission
            Could only be to restore my dear
                Homeland to the German Reich.
I have believed in this mission, I have lived
        And fought for it, and I believe
            I have now fulfilled it.

'I CAN ONLY DESCRIBE HIM, AS BEING IN
A STATE OF ECSTACY'
'I CAN ONLY DESCRIBE HIM, AS BEING IN
A STATE OF ECSTACY'   (Papen)

Certain foreign newspapers have said that
        We fell on Austria with brutal methods.
                I can only say:

Even in death they cannot stop lying.
I have in the course of my political struggle
Won much love from my people,
But when I crossed the former frontier
There met much stream of love
As I have never experienced.
Not as tyrants have we come,
As liberators.
Under the force of this impression
I decided not to wait until
April tenth but to affect the unification
Forthwith. . .
I believed that it was God's will to send
A youth from here Into the Reich,
To let him grow up, to raise him
to be the leader of the nation so as
To enable him to lead the homeland
Into the Reich.
There are higher ordering and we all are
Nothing else than agents.
When on March 9 Herr Schuschnigg broke
His agreement, then in that second
I felt that now the call of Providence
Had come to me, and that which
Took place in three days was only
Conceivable as the fulfillment
Or the wish and the will of this Providence.
In three days the Lord has smitten them!
. . . And to me the grace was giving

On the day of the betrayal to be able
To unite my homeland with the Reich!
I would now give thanks
        Let me return to my homeland
In order that I might now lead into
        My German Reich! Tomorrow
May every German recognize the hour
        And measure its import and how
Its humility before the Almighty,
Who in a few weeks has wrought
        A miracle upon us!
Himmler arrested 79,000 'unreliables'
In the first few weeks surrounding
        Hitler visit, 14 March.
Karl Adolf Eichmann became administer
        Of the 'Office of Jewish Emigration',
Set up by Heydrich. A concentration camp
Was erected in Mauthausen,
        Near Enns.

These became instruments
        Of extermination.
35,318 officially listed executions
In six and a half years.

ANSWER: 'YES' OR 'NO' TO THE PLEBISCITE.
'YES' CONTINUE, ELSE

Seig Hitler! Heil! Hitler!
Hang Schuschnigg!

LIKE THIS POET WHO ANSWERED 'NO';
YOU WILL BE CONFINED AND IMPRISIONED.

AND ALL MEN SHALL HATE EACH OTHER.

THE END OF PART THREE.

PART FOUR

THE NEW ORDER

'untermenschen'
'What happen to a Russian and a Czech,
Does not interest me in the slightest,'
Declared Heinrich Himmler, 4 October, 1943. . .
'What the nations can offer in the way
Of the good blood of our type,
We will take, if necessary, by kidnapping
Their children and raising them here with us.
Whether nations live in prosperity
Or starve to death interest me in so far
As we need them as slaves
To our Kultur.
Otherwise, it is of no interest to me.
Whether 10,000 Russian females fall down
From exhaustion while digging
An antitank ditch interest me only
In so far as the antitank ditch
for Germany is finished. . .'

Jacques Roux, on the rostrum on the Convention,
25 June 1793: Liberty is no more than
An empty shell when one class of men
Is allowed to condemn another
To starvation without any measure
Being taken against them.
And equally is also an empty when the rich,

By exercising their economic monopolies
Have the power of life or death
Over other members of the community.'
'Make your decision and the san-culottes,
With their pikes in their hands
Will see that your decrees are duly enforced.'

THE EXTRAORDINARY CRIMINAL TRIBUNAL.

Erich Koch, the Ukraine Reich Commissar,
2 March, 1943:
'We are the Master Race and must govern
Hard but just. . .I will draw the very last out
of this country. I did not come to spread bliss
. . .The population must work, work, and
Work again. . .We definitely not come here
To give out manna. We have come
Here to create the basis for victory,
We are the master race, which must
Remember that the lowest German worker
Is radically and biologically a thousand
Times more valuable than the population here.'
Martin Gorman, Hitler's party secretary:
The Slavs are to work for us.
In so far as we don't need them,
They may die. Therefore compulsory
Vaccination and German health service
Are superfluous. The fertility

Of the slave is undesirable.
They may use contraceptives or
        practice abortion---the more the better.
Education is dangerous. It is enough
        If they can count to a 100. . .
Every educated person is a future enemy.
Religion leave to them as a means to diversion.
        As for food they won't get anymore
        Then absolutely necessary.
We are the masters, we come first.

The Insurrectionary Commune of 10 August
        Imprisoned Louis XVI and his family
In the Temple and placed it under guard.
Judges would be elected by the Paris sections
        Which would have power to prosecute
In cases of counterrevolutionary offences.
        And that public official,
        As well as priests, must pledge an oath
                Of loyalty to the principals
Of liberty and equality.
        A house-to-house search
                Was granted for arms
        That might be in possession of those
Who might be suspect to be
                Counterrevolutionaries.

First I went to a shuttle bus
        But was approached by a gentleman
who said a taxi to hotel
        would be 150 crowns.
    I decided it was better to leave at once,
and it was less expensive
                then I thought it would be
        I was directed to a cab driver
                Who would take me
                (he spoke a little English).
    He was a delightful man
            Who spoke highly of his country
'Food is good, cheap, and the hotels are nice.
    The country is a very beautiful place,
        That is why you have returned.'
The driver pointed to the new hotel Forum
        Near Gottwaldova Metro Station.
    First, I must say, that we came by
        The Summer Palace on Marianske hradby
The USA Embassy is passed and always
Pointed out (a place where I avoid,
        Remembering Budapest)
Then along the nabe. Kpt. Jarose
        In order to avoid traffic
Of the center (centrum) of the city,
. . . Then the driver asked me exchange money
        But I always refuse, before the hotel.
        The black market is annoying
When one first arrives one reads that it can be

Sort of a test by loyal citizens.
Yet the government is in need of hard currency
And so do those who wish to buy
Foreign goods at their Tuzex stores.
I arrived in Panorama hotel
Which is south of centrum
I entered this modern hotel, and
My bags placed in a cart
By a porter. Then my reservations verified
On one of the computers.
One leaves passport for night
And is led by porter
To a very comfortable room.
Too late to go downtown
To the Reiseboro of DDR.
I took a bath and rest before dinner.
I had bohemian goulash.
There were two restaurants, a café,
A snack bar, disco in the hotel.

Whenever you come across anything that
May be needed by the German people,
You must be after it like a bloodhound.
It must be taken out . . .
Brought to Germany.
(Goering)
First to dominate it, second to administer it,

Third to exploit it. . .it enables us
To eradicate everyone who oppose us.
Hitler—
'Poland can only be administered
By utilizing the country
Through means of ruthless exploitation,
Deportation of all the supplies,
Raw materials, machines,
Factory installations etc. . . . .
Which are important for the German war
Economy, availability of all workers
For work within Germany,
Reduction of entire Polish economy
To absolute minimum be necessary
Bare existence of the population,
Closing of all educational institutions,
Especially technical schools and colleges
In order to prevent the growth
Of the new Polish intelligencia,
Poland shall be treated as a colony.
The Poles shall be the slaves
Of the Greater German Reich.'
Dr. Frank informed the Army of Hitler's orders.

More than eleven hundred prisoners were executed.
. . .the Comite de Surveillance: 'this course of action
Which is so necessary if public security
Is to be ensured. . .'retaining by a policy

of terror the loyalty the great legions
Of traitors who lie hidden within our walls
At a moment when the people
Are about to March against the enemy.'

It is no longer a question of making a choice
Between order and disorder,
But between the new regime and the old,
For behind the foreign armies are lurking
The emigres on the frontiers.
The sense of shock is profound, especially
Among those classes of society
Which alone carried the full weight
Of the former structure,
Among the millions of men who scratched
A meager living by manual labor. . .
Who, taxed, pillaged and bullied for centuries,
Suffered misery, oppression, and
Contempt from generation to generation.
They know their own bitter experiences
How much their present condition
Differs from that they have known
Until recently. They have only to cast their minds
Back to recall the full enormity of the tax
Burden they bore, whether in dues to the King,
To the Church, or to the seigneurs.
A formidable anger is spreading
from the workshop to the cottage.
An anger that finds expression

in the nationalist songs
Which denounce the conspiracy of tyrants
Of Europe and call the people to arms.
-Hippolyte Trine-

"I cannot remember everything!
I must have been conscious most of the time!
****Music August 27, 1988; 20:48 ****

The wild and ruthless manhunt,
as exercised everywhere
in towns and country, in streets, squares, stations,
Even in churches, at night in homes,
Has badly shaken the feeling of security
Of the inhabitants.
Everybody is exposed to the danger
Of being seized anywhere and
Anytime by the police,
Suddenly and unexpectedly,
And being sent to an assembly camp.
None of his relatives knew what had happened to him.
(A German officer to Governor Frank.)
Because of corpses the trainload of returning
Laborers a catastrophe might
Have occurred. . . In the train
Women gave birth to babies
That were thrown out the windows
During the journey.
Persons having tuberculosis and venereal diseases

Rode in the same car.
Dying people in freight cars without straw,
And one of the dead was thrown
on a railway embankment.
The sand must have occurred in other
Returning transports.
(Dr. Gutkelch in a report to ministry.)

Upon my first visit I found these females
Open festering wounds and other diseases.
I was, the first doctor they had seen
In at least a fortnight . . .
There were no medical supplies. . .
They had no shoes and went about
In their bare feet. The sole clothing
Of each consisted of a sack with holes
For their arms and head.
Their hair was shorn.
The camp was surrounded by barbed wire
And closely guarded by SS guards.
The amount of food in the camp
was extremely meagre and very poor quality.
One could not enter the barracks
Without being attacked by fleas. . .
I got large boils on my arms and
the rest of my body from them. . .
(Dr. Jaeger to the directors of Kripp.)

The clothing of the Eastern workers
    Likewise, completely inadequate.
They worked and slept in the same clothing
      In which they arrived from the East.
Virtually all of them had no overcoats
And were compelled to use their blankets
    As coats in cold and rainy weather.
In view of the shortage of shoes many
     Workers were forced to go to work
       In their bare feet in winter. . .
Sanitary conditions were atrocious.
At Kramerplatz only ten children's toilets
     Were available for 1,200 inhabitants
    . . . The Tartars and Kirghiz suffered most;
They collapsed like flies from bad housing,
      The poor quality and insufficient
     Quantity of food, overwork and
  Insufficient rest.
     These workers were likewise affiliated
With spotted fever. Like the carrier of diseases,
    Together with countless fleas, bugs
     And other vermin tortured
   The inhabitants of these camps. . .
At times the water supply at the camps
    Was shut off for periods of eight to
     Fourteen days. . .
It's inhabitants were kept in for nearly
   For nearly half a year in dog kennels,
     Urinals, and in an old baking house.

The dog kennels were three feet high,
Nine feet long, six feet wide.
                    Five men slept in each of them.
The prisoners had to crawl into these
                    Kennels on all fours. . .
There was no water in the camp.
                    (Dr. Jeager's report)
From workers of Polish nationality
                    No longer have right to complain,
And thus, now no complains will be accepted
                    By the official agency. . .
The visit of churches is strictly prohibited. . .
                    Visits to theaters, motion pictures
                    Or other cultural entertainment
                    Are strictly prohibited . . .
Sexual intercourse with women and girls
                    Is strictly prohibited.
Arbitrary change of employment
                    Is strictly prohibited.
The farm workers have to labor as long
                    As is demanded by employer.
                    There are no time limits to working time.
                    Every employer has the right to give
Corporal punishment to his farmworkers. . .
                    They should, if possible, be removed
From the community of the home
                    And can be quartered in stables, etc.
No remorse should restrict such action.
                    (A directive, 6, March 1941.)

I enjoy the Bohemian one,
   Because they had Gypsy music
 The same band as two years ago.
The food in socialist Europe
   Is much better than many
  Of the restaurants in Cherry Hill
 I believe that many Americans
   Do not know what good food is.
In Magyar Napkoztarszag (Hungary)
  I have purchased in many foods stores
   When I rented rooms with families.
I saw only one line in Erfurt (DDR)
   ! did not even bother to go into the market
  In Berlin (DDR), for I have seen
The one in Budapest,
    which was filled with food.
With the jet lag, I decided to watch TV
    And go to bed early.
  Television is quite interesting
  Much better than
public television network in our country.
   One may also get Soviet, Polish,
And one DDR station.
  There are many Czech stations.
On Soviet TV there are many interviews
   With citizens, at work and home.
Something that is uncommon
  on our star-studded Hollywood TV shows
   and Capitalist networks.

There is more classical music than PBC, also
   Popular music shows were very common
In DDR, and Rock music is very popular
   Something the Capitalist like to deny.
After breakfast, a buffet for 50 K,
   I had nine 50 K coupons
   My half board, I walked to the Metro,
   Past the Motokov building
Which is taller, and even more modern.
It is a motor vehicle manufacture,
   Trucks, tractors etc.
   The station that one enters
Is Mladeznicka, which has an escalator,
   As all others. It cost 1K
One buy ones ticket from a vending machine.
   The first line opened in May 1974
   With Soviet co-cooperation.
It is nicer than our modern High-Speed line
   That takes commutes into center city
   Philadelphia.

The first stop is Gottwaldova,
Named after the first Communists leader,
   Klement Gottwald.
The usual stop is Muzem
   Where the National Museum
   Is located.
On the highest point on Vaclavska nam.
A main shopping boulevard

Which is very beautiful.
The center is a walk with flowers
And trees.
This is one of the busiest, cafes, cinemas, discos
And widest streets; stores, a few airlines.
The opposite end of the boulevard,
Is a pedestrian street; Na prikope
Which leads to the Powder Tower,
And Narodni. . .which leads to the most
1 Maji (bridge) and the National Theater.
I walk past the Mustek station of Metro B and
Entered the square that begins
The pedestrian street. Ice cream,
Is very popular and the is many places to get a cone.
One strolls the crowded street
Filled with people eating ice cream.
I walked hastily toward the Powder Tower,
And then to the square where
The old Town Hall is then to Parizaka street
Where the Reiseboro is.

THE BATLE OF VALMY

The Prussian advance and capture Verdun,
2 September; royalist murdered
lieutenant-colonel, Beaurepaire,
Of the battalion of Maine-et Loire.
The enemy reached the Argonne, 8 September,

Encounted and the French army.
Yet an Austrian detachment forced
Its way through the mountain pass
At La Croix-aux-Bois on the 12th.
The way to Paris seemed opened.
Kellerman and his army joined Dumouriez,
On thee 19th. 50,000 French
Verses 34,000 Royalists. Kellerman
Took his hat, stuck in on sword waving and
Shouting 'Long live the nation',
And the sans-culottes fired.
the cannon fire continued till
The evening, than a rainstorm broke.

GOETHE WAS PRESENT, AND ENGRAVED
ARE HIS WORDS:
'This day and this place open a new era
In the history of the world.'

Paris must suffer a high loss of influence
So that it enjoys one-eighty-third
Of the power of the nation. . .
Just like another department'.
(Lasource)
'The party. . .whose intention it is to set up
A dictatorship is the party of Robespierre.'
(Rebecqui)
I think that I am the first political writer,

And perhaps the only man in France
Since the Revolution, to propose
           a military tribunal, a dictator,
And a trium-virates as the only possible
                Of crushing traitors. . .
       Three years in prisons and torments,
Three years he suffered
                To save his country.
       And this is the result of all my efforts,
My labors, so much too my agony, my
                Sufferings, and
           The dangers which I have run!
Ah, well! I stay in your midst to brave
                Your anger too!   (Marat)
'Robespierre, I accuse you of having continually
Sought the plaudits of the crowd and
           Of having set yourself up as an object
Of idiolatry, I accuse you of having
           Tyrannized the electoral assembly
Of the Department of Paris by all the methods
Of intrigue and terror at your disposal;
           And finally, I accuse you of having
Quite obviously set your sights
On a position of supreme power. (Louver)
'I do not see myself as a defendant
       But as a defender of the cause
                Patriotism. . .
Far from being personally ambitious,
I have always fought against those who have

Been motivated by a desire
For self-advancement.'
                              (Robespierre)
'All those things were illegal, as illegal as
              As the Revolution itself,
The overthrow of the throne and
              The storming of the Bastille,
       As illegal as liberty itself.
It is impossible to want a revolution
       Without having revolutionary action.'
                              (Robespierre)

The capitalist police held me overnight,
       In 1982, in municipal jail.
              In the morning I was arraigned
Without a lawyer.
              Transferred to the overcrowded
County jail,
                     a large room with young men
              Sleeping on floor.
A 20-inch television (propaganda)
              Blurred above in the front.
Refusing to give information
                     To prisoners and cooperate.
I was attacked, pushed into a double cell
       My testicles were grabbed,
              As I placed my arm against his neck,
His head between the bars,
              As I called for the guards.

Receiving stitches in the head above the eye.
I was transferred to the State Psychiatric prison.

As for the ridiculous hundred Slavs,
We will mold the best of them
To the shape that suits us,
And we will isolate the rest of them
In their own pigsties;
And anyone who talks about cherishing
The local inhabitant and civilizing him,
Goes straight off to a concentration camp!
-Hitler, July 1941.

All the Jews and communist functionaries
Were removed from prisoner-of-war camps
And were executed.
To my knowledge this action carried out
The entire Russian campaign. . .
(Ohlendorf)

This order is intended for commanders only
And must not under any circumstances
Fall into enemy hands.'
The Einsatz unit would enter a village or town
And order the prominent Jewish citizens
To call together all Jews for the purpose
Of 'resettlement.'
They were requested to hand over

Their valuables and shortly before
Execution to surrender their outer clothing.
They were transported to the place of executions,
Usually an antitank ditch,
In trucks—always only as many as
Could be executed immediately.
In this way it was attempted to keep
The span of time from moment
In which the victims knew what it was about
To happen to them until time
Of actual execution as a short as possible.
Then they were shot, knelling or standing
By firing squads in a military manner
And corpes throw into a ditch.   (Ohlendorf)

The troublemakers are those who want to
Level everything down ---
Properly, human comfort, the price of goods,
And the various services that are performed
For for society.   (Brissot)

Royalty has been destroyed, the nobility
And the clergy have disappeared
And now the reign of equality is beginning . . .
Who want to build a Republic
Only to suit themselves and their interest
Whose intention it is to govern.
In the interest of the rich and the public officials.
(Robespierre)

Those who gave us the theoretical basis
        For our society did not consider
Those goods which are necessary
        To keep people alive as anything
Other than an ordinary item of trade;
They discerned no difference between
        Trading corn and trading in indigo;
They talked as much greater length
        About the mechanics of corn trade
Than about the subsistence of the people.
        They treated with great consideration
The profits that accrued to the merchants
And landowners but laid little or
        No store by the value of human life.
The very first right of all is the right to exist.
        The first law society is therefore that
Which guarantees all its members the means
        Whereby they can continue to stay alive;
        All other laws are subordinate
                To that law. (Robespierre)

My directions now have proved that the correct
        Adjustment of the levels of death
Comes faster and prisoners fall asleep peacefully.
        Disordered faces and excretions,
Such as could be seen before,
        are no longer noticed.
                (Dr Becker)

THE TRIAL OF LOUIS XVI

The same men who about to judge Louis
    Have another task to perform
    They have a republic to found. And those
       Who attach any importance to meting
Out justice to a king will never found
      A republic. As for myself I do not see
The possibility of a middle way:
      This man must reign or he must die. . .
It is not possible to rule in perfect innocence,
        And the sheer folly of such an idea

Is only too obvious. All kings are rebels
      And usurpers.
    (Saint-Just; 13 November 1792)

He is the murderer of the Bastille, of Nancy
      And the Champ-de-Mars,
    Of Tournay and the Tuileries.
What foreigner or which of your enemies
      Has done you greater harm?
        (Saint-Just)

The King is not a defendant, and you are not
      Judges. You do not have to decide
In favor of a man or against him.
What you have to do is to take a step that will
      Benefit public safety, to adopt

A measure that will safeguard
The nation.   (Robespierre)
The proposal that the King be tried at all,
By whatever means, is a step backwards
Towards royal and constitutional despotism.
It is a counter-revolutionary idea,
For it puts the Revolution itself in the dock.
(Robespierre)

Is Louis Capet guilty of conspiring against liberty
Of the people and of trying to undermine
The security of the State?
Will the sentence that is passed
Be referred back to the people
For ratification?

What should be the penalty inflicted on Louis?
(14 January 1793; National Convention)

THE EXECUTION OF LOUIS XVI; 21 January, 1793.

THE EXECUTION OF LOUIS XVI

THE EXECUTION OF LOUIS XVI; 21 January 1793.

THE EXECUTION OF LOUIS XVI

We are fully committed now.
The paths have been cut off behind
Us and we have no choice but to go forward
Whether we like it or not.
Now as never before we can truly say
That we shall live as free men or die.
-20 January, Lebas

AND ALL MEN SHALL HATE EACH OTHER.

THE END OF PART FOUR

PART FIVE

THE FINAL SOLUTION

THE FINAL SOLUTION

THE FINAL SOLUTION

Today, the twenty-third of October 1988.
    I have reached a final solution.
       It is eight months from the day
   I wrote of a 'new' life.
         It has been a productive eight months,
And I feel that I have stumbled on a solution.
No longer will waste my efforts, bourgeois women
    Are only interested in money.
The proletariat-capitalist women only
    Interested in the 'fashionable male.
The present tactics of Communist party USA
    Are a mistake. Its approach, restricts
Itself with the 'fashionable'. The party tries to
    Out guess the working class, and
  the bourgeois intellectuals,
      into knowing how they think.
It plays on the superficial premise,
    Adopting this view or that,
      Feigning to be popular.
A large percentage of the masses now reject

'liberalism', as the result of the Carter
Administration. Associating oneself with
An unpopular cause, the majority
Of Americans don't vote, and majority
Of those who voted, rejected
'Carterism' twice. The bankruptcy of his policies,
And the hypocrisy of his 'human rights' and
His 'anti-communist actions',
Left many 'progressives' and 'moderates'
With a bitter taste of the capitalist
'bourgeois' liberalism.

I am very happy 'improving' my living conditions.
The enjoyment of classical music,
Is invigorating. I have returned to studying
The piano, though Rutgers
In Camden is a typical capitalist university,
Like Temple, in Philadelphia.
I have no hope for advancement at work,
I can little by little make myself self-sufficient.
I am against making male friends,
And against rejoining the literary world.
Much happiness can be achieved without
These distractions, and I can develop on my own.
Pat Oxley has written me in kindness,
Urging me to follow my own judgements and
Ignore the literary establishment.
Though this is always my belief, it is nice to hear
Someone reinforces this.

I can no longer subscribe to her journal
Because of its poor quality.
Eight years ago I should have printed a good
Black and white version of THE ANTI-CHRIST.
One local bookmaker has refused
to print my book for its content.
I have also tried a large one out of state,
But it would not also print the text.

June 1946; Nuremberg,
Three American prosecution staff
Questioned
S.S. Obergruppenfueher Oswald Pohl,
In charge of work projects inmates
Of Nazi concentration camps.
And what was that? Pohl was asked.
'The extermination of Jewry,' he answered.

I here with commission you
(Goering instructed Heydrich)
To carry out all preparations with regard to
A total solution of the Jewish question in
In those territories of Europe
Which are under German influence.
I furthermore charge you to submit to me
As soon as possible a draft showing the . . .
Measures already taken for the execution

The intended final solution
            Of the Jewish question.
If the international Jewish financiers . . .
            Again, succeed in plunging
The nations into the world war
            The result will be. . .
The annihilation of the Jewish race
            Throughout Europe.
            (Adolf Hitler, 30 Jan., 1939)

The Jews should now In the course
            of the final solution be brought to the East
. . . For use as labor. In big labor gangs,
            With separation of sexes, the Jews
Capable of work are brought to these areas
            And employed in road building,
In which task undoubtedly a great part
            Will fall through natural diminution.
The remnant that finally is able to survive all this
            --since this undoubtedly the part
With the strongest resistance---
Must be treated accordingly, since these people
            Representing a natural selection,
Are to be regarded as the germ cell
            A new Jewish development.
                        (Heydrich)
I also want to talk to you quite frankly
            On a very grave matter.

Among ourselves it should be mentioned
            quite frankly, and we never speak
Of it publicly. . . I mean. . .
The extermination of the Jewish race. . .
Most of you must know what it means when
            100 corpses are lying side by side,
Or 500 or 1000. To have stuck it out
            And at the same time---
Apart from exceptions caused by human weakness---
            To have remained decent fellows,
                    That is what has made us hard.
This is page in glory in our history
            Which has never been written
And never to be written. . .   (Himmler)

The 'Final Solution' of the Jewish question
            Meant the complete extermination
Of all Jews In Europe. I was ordered
To establish extermination facilities at Auschwitz
            In June 1941.
At that time there were already
            In the General Government of Poland
Three other extermination camps:
            Belzec, Treblink and Wolzek.
I visited Treblinka to find out how they
            Carried out their extermination.
The camp commandant at Treblinka
            Told me that he had liquated
                    80,000 in the course of a half year.

He was principally concerned with liquating
                    All the Jews from the Warsaw ghetto.
He used monoxide gas and I did not think
                    That his methods were very efficient.
So when I set up the extermination building
                    At Auschwitz, I used Zyklon B,
        Which was a crystallized prussic acid
Which we dropped into the death chamber
                    From a small opening.
It took three to fifteen minutes
                    to kill the people in death chamber,
        Depending on climate conditions.
We knew when the people were dead
                    Because the screaming stopped.
        We usually waited a half hour
                    Before opening the doors
        And moved the bodies.
                    After the bodies were removed
        Our special commandos took off
        The rings and extracted the gold
                    From the teeth of the corpses.
Another improvement we made over Treblinka
        Was that we built our gas chambers
To accommodate 2,000 people at one time,
        Whereas at Treblinka their ten gas chambers
                    Only accommodated 200 people each.
                            (Rudolf Hoess)

Still another improvement we made over Treblinka
        Was that at Treblinka the victims
        Almost always knew that they were
                To be exterminated,
        At Auschwitz we endeavored to fool
        The victims into thinking they
        Were to go through a delousing process.
Of course, frequently they realized our true
        Intensions, and we sometimes
                Had riots and difficulties.
        Very frequently women hide their children
        Under clothes but of course when
                We found them we would send
        The children in to be exterminated
        We were required to carry out
                these exterminations in secrecy,
But of course, the foul and nauseating stench
        From the continuous burning of bodies
                Permeated the entire area
        And all the people living in the surrounding
                Communities knew the exterminations
Were going on in Auschwitz.   (Rudolf Hoess)

    WALDSEE
We were doing very well here
We have work and we are all well treated
We await your arrival.

Their first task was to remove the blood
And defecations before dragging
The clawing dead apart with nooses and hooks,
The prelude to the ghastly search for gold
And removal of teeth and hair were regarded
By the Germans as strategic materials.
Then the journey by lift or rail-wagon
To the furnaces, the mill that ground
The clinker to fine ash, and the truck
That scattered the ashes in the steam
Of the Sola.   (Reitlinger)

Following our verbal discussion regarding
        The delivery of equipment of simple
Construction for the burning of bodies,
        We are submitting plans for
        Our perfected cremation ovens
Which operate with coal and in which
        Hitherto given full satisfaction.

We suggest two crematoria furnaces
        For the building planned, but we advice you
                To make further inquires to make sure
That the two ovens will be sufficient
                For your requirements.
        We guarantee the effectiveness
                Of the cremation ovens as well as
        Their durability, the use of the best

Material and our faultless workmanship.
            Awaiting your further word.
            We will be at your service.
            Heil Hitler!

            C. H. KORI, G. B. H.

We all knew that these places were sites
            Of concentration camps.
            It was in the tenth delivery in November 1943,
That dental gold appeared.
            The quantity of dental gold
                        became unusually great.
In this conversation no doubt remained
            That the objects to be delivered
            Came from the Jews who had been killed
                        In the concentration camps.
The objects I question were rings, watches,
            Eyeglasses, gold bars, wedding rings,
            Bracelets, puns, gold fillings and other valuables.

Ten years have passed since I began
                        the actual writing of the present poem
            Of which this is an introduction.
The original type is in four colors
            (Red, green, blue, brown) and black.
            What this introduces is a black and white
                        Version which is more economical.
The poem THE ANTI-CHRIST was written one page

At a time, taking approximately
One week per page.
The original plan was written in March 1975,
After completing my satirical poetic drama
Or libretto JASON (1973-1974).
It was published the following year
In LITTACK in England,
And is here enclosed.
My last original work to be printed.
The title of the poem is its
three most important words.
The initials of the next Presidents name,
Played a part in the choice of the title.
The effects of thus degenerate hypocrite
Can still be felt some three elections after.
The first eleven pages were taped I July 1978,
And broadcast in August 1978.
I sold my home, after completing thirty-nine pages,
And embarked on the extensive trip
To Eastern Europe which was aborted.

In May I arrived in Warsaw, but had to go straight
to Budapest by train
because I was convinced by a bank
In South Jersey that money
could be easily transferred.
I embarked before my home was sold.
This was my fourth visit to Hungary,
And the contrast to 1975, my first,

Had become apparent.
While economically improvement blossomed,
A large debt accumulated.
Owning large sums to capitalist banks
And institutions. The ruling class still restricted
Democratic involvement.
The economic miracle came to a 'slow down'.
Most Americans know through experience
That capitalist banks are often
Bureaucratic and incompetent.
I received a bank check rather than
An international money order,
And a responding telex arrived
twenty-seven days later,
Which should have taken four days.
Restaurants which were privately owned refused
My receipt from the Hungarian National Bank.
One state owned one that I frequented,
Gave me goulash and soup.
Therefore, after seven days without eating
I regained my strength.
The American Embassy also would not help
Or honor my note.
They are only there for diplomat reasons.
In the summer of 1980, I attempted to make
At my expense.
The enclosed poem, in its original format,
Though in black and white,
A deck of cards. I was shortly after

Warned by the Secret Service
Of Philadelphia.
I was asked to give a reading in Philadelphia,
But that was suddenly cancelled.
I was arrested after a few pranks phone calls
To the headquarters.
I thought a few weeks in prisons
Might be educational.

Hardly had the operation had begun,
Then we ran into-strong concerted
Fire by the Jews and bandits.
The tank and two armored cars
Pelted with Molotov cocktails. . .
Owing to this enemy counterattack
We had to withdraw.
About 1730 hours we encountered
Very strong resistance from a block of buildings,
Including machine-gun fire.
A special raiding party defeated the enemy
But could not catch the resistors.
The Jews and criminals resisted from
Base to base and escaped at the last moment.
. . . Our losses in the first attack: 12 men.
Within a few days it became apparent
That the Jews no longer had any intention
To resettle voluntarily,
But were determined to resist evacuation

. . . Whereas it had been possible during the first days
　　　　　To catch considerable number of Jews,
　　　Who are cowards by nature, it became
　　　　　More and more difficult during
　　　The second half of the operation
　　　　　to capture the bandits and Jews.
Over and over again new battle groups
　　　Consisting of 20 to 30 Jewish men,
Accompanied by corresponding number
　　　Of women. Kindled new resistance.
　　　　　　　　　(S.S. General Stroop)

I therefore decided to destroy the entire
　　　Jewish area by setting every block
　　　　　On fire.
The Jews stayed in the burning buildings
　　　　　Until because of the fear
　　　Of being burned alive they jumped
From the upper stories. . .with their
　　　　　Bones broken they tried to crawl
Across the street into the building
Which had not been yet set on fire. . .
　　　Despite the danger of being burned
　　　　　Alive the Jews and the bandits
Often preferred to return into the flames
　　　Rather than risk being caught by us.

I am going to try to obtain a train for T2
　　　(Treblinka) tomorrow.

Otherwise, liquidation will be carried out
Here tomorrow.
During the day several more blocks of buildings
Were burned down.
This is the only and final method which
Forces this trash and sub humanity
To the surface. (S.S. General Stroop)

THE WARSAW GHETTO IS NO MORE

THE WARSAW GHETTO IS NO MORE

THE WARSAW GHETTO IS

Jewish quarter of Warsaw is no longer In existence.
The large—scale action was terminated
At 2015 hours by blowing up
the Warsaw synagogue.
Total number of Jews dealt with 56,055,

Including Jews caught and Jews whose
Extermination can be proved.

Of the total of the 56,055 caught, about 7,000
Were destroyed in former ghetto
During large-scale operation, 6,929 Jews
Were destroyed by transporting them
To Treblinka; the total Jews destroyed
Is therefore 13,929.

Beyond that from five to six thousand
Jews were destroyed by being blown up
Or perishing in flames.
                    (S.S. General Stroop)

I was immediately arraigned in Federal court
In Camden, not able to procure
$200,000.00 bail.
The Secret Services stated in court
That they had tapes of me threatening
The President, the great champion of Human Rights.
No tapes ever existed, and I therefore
Refused to plea guilty. I had no consul,
And was given a unreasonable bail,
And shipped to Springfield, Missouri,
In a Federal Medical prison
After a few days in Trenton State.
The impression of this institution is vivid,
People with one arm or one leg.
In the recreation field. I could not stand
Trial till I was fit. Eventually after finally getting
A Federal defender, I convinced him while
I was in New York City Federal prison,
That he should challenge the Secret Services
Boast of having tapes. . .
'Let them produce them'.
They never did it was judged unfit for trial.
Despite my defender's outrage,

I was transferred to the local level,
Where eventually charges were dropped,
On inaugural day 1981.
This all lasted six months after I was denied
A reasonable bail.
The attempts to remove me from my inheritance
Property, at work, and the smashing
Of my house window, have been
A few of the benevolent actions
Of the Cherry Hill Police.
These actions were necessary due to my
Insanity, for we know that there are none
That there are no dissidents in
The United States who are mistreated,
Jailed, or confined to a mental institution.

While waiting for LOT office to open (Polish airlines),
In early August 1979. I sat in a park,
And I was arrested, though
Not handcuffed. I therefore regretted
The confrontation with U. S. Embassy,
I was expelled for carrying Communist Propaganda.
The last ten pages were written
In Hungary, and typed up
At my grandfather's in Tuscany, Italy.
This is important for the poem
must not be associated with any government.
The poem is satirical and parodic response
To Anti-Communist propaganda,

And undemocratic socialism.
Important to the change in tone, from the placid
Plans of 1975, is the or wholesale
Reproduction of the 1909 copyright law
Which made all books not copyrighted
Before 1979 public domain.
Some parts of poem are fiction,
Other parts are based on reality.
The words 'A falu' in Hungarian mean 'a folk tale'
Or 'story'. The story is that of a white male
Who meets a Afro-American girl,
Before their marriage the CIA
Gives the young man 'electric shock treatment'
For his involvement in Anti-Vietnam demonstrations.
Therefore, it is only six years later
That they are reunited.

In 1986, I was again able to leave the state and
Return to Czechoslovakia.
In 1987, I was again not permitted to leave
New Jersey, I returned again, in 1988,
While I was traveling sixteen days in the DDR.
I have been informed many times,
That it was a nice place to visit
But you would not want to live there.

I only hope that someday my dream will not
Become true. That I may be caged
Like an animal, and brought back

America to be confined for
13 years in St. Elizabeth's Hospital,
As Ezra Pound.

The thought alone that three million Bolsheviks
Now in German captivity could
Be sterilized, so that they would be available
For work but precluded from propaganda,
Opens up the most far-reaching perspectives

THE MEDICAL EXPERIMENTS

I had no feeling in carrying out these things
Because I had received an order
To kill the eighty inmates in the way
I already told you.
That, by the way, was the way I was trained.
(An Assistant)
Can you make available two or three professional
Criminals for these experiments. . .
The experiments, by which the subjects
Can of course die, would take place with
My co-operation.   (Dr. Rascher)
The third test was without oxygen
At the equivalent of 29,400 feet aptitude
Conducted on a 37-year old Jew
In good general condition.
Respiration continued for 30 minutes.

After four minutes the TP (test person)
Began to perspire and roll his head.
After five minutes spasms appeared,
Between the sixth and tenth minute
Respiration increased in frequently,
The TP losses consciousness.
From the eleventh to thirteenth minute
Respiration slowed down
To three per minute.
Only to cease entirely at the end of that period.
. . . About a half a hour after breathing had ceased,
An autopsy was begun.
I have personally seen through the observation
Window of the decompression chamber
When a prisoner inside would stand a vacuum
Until the lungs ruptured. . .
They would go mad and pull out their hair
In an effort to relieve the pressure.
They would tear their heads and face
With their fingers and nails
In an attempt to maim themselves
In their madness. They would beat
The walls with their head and scream
In an effort to relieve the pressure
On their eardrums. These cases usually
Ended the death of the subject.
The TP were immersed in water in full flying
Uniform. . . with hood.
A life jacket prevented sinking. The experiments

Were conducted at water temperatures
Between 36.5- and 53.5-degrees Fahrenheit.
In the first test series the back of the head
And brain stem were above water.
In another series the back of the neck and
The brain were above water.
In another the back of the neck and cerebellum
Were submerged. Temperatures
as low as 79.5 in the stomach
And 79.7 in the rectum were recorded electrically.
Fatalities occurred only when medulla
And the cerebellum were chilled.
In autopsies of such fatality's large quantities
Of free blood, up to a pint, were always
Found inside the cranial cavity.
The heart regularly showed extreme distention
Of the right chamber. The TPs in such
Test inevitability died when body temperature
Had declined to 82.5, despite
All rescue attempts.
The autopsy findings proved the important of
A heated head and neck protector
For the foam suit now in the process
Of development.
It was the worst experiment ever made.
Two Russian officers were brought
From the prison barracks.
Rancher has them stripped and they
Had to go into a vat naked.

Hour after hour went by, and whereas usually
Unconsciousness from the cold
Set in after sixty minutes at latest,
The two men in this case still responded
Fully after two and a half hours.
All appeals to Rascher to out them to sleep
By injection were fruitless.
About the third hour one of the Russians
Said to the other:
'Comrade tell the officer to shoot us'
The other replied that he expected no mercy
From this Fascist dog.
The two shook hands with a 'Farewell. Comrade'
. . . These words were translated to Rascher
By a young Pole, though in somewhat
Different form.
Rascher went to his office.
The young Pole at once tried to chloroform
The two victims,
but Rascher came back at once,
Threatening us with a gun.
The test lasted at least five hours
before death supervened.

The test persons were chilled in the familiar
Way---dressed or undressed---
In cold water at various temperatures. . .
Removal from the water took place at rectal
Temperature of 86 degrees.

In eight test persons were placed
    Between two naked women on a wide bed.
The women were instructed to snuggle up to
    The chilled person as closely as possible.
The three persons were then covered with blankets.
        . . .Once the test persons regained
Consciousness, they never lost it again,
                quickly grasping
        Their situation and nestling close
            To the naked bodies of the women.
The rise of the body temperature then proceeded
        At approximately the same speed
        As with the test persons warmed by
        Being swathed in his blankets. . .
An exception was formed by four test persons
        Who practiced sexual intercourse
            Between 86.5 and 89.5 degrees,
In these persons, after coitus, a very swift
        Temperature rises ensued, comparable

To that achieved by means of a hot-water bath.
                (Dr. Rascher)

THE ASSASSINATION OF REINHARD HEYDRICH

The chief of the Chief of the Security Police
    And the S.D., Deputy chief of Ge(heime)
        Sta(ate) po(lizei): GESTAPO.

'Hangman Heydrich', as he became known
Reinhard Heydrich became the Acting Protector
Of Bohemia and Moravia,
In September 1941.
While driving his Mercedes convertible
From his country villa
to the Hradschin Castle
In Prague, a bomb, made in Britain,
Was thrown; his car was totally destroyed
And his spine was shattered.
Two members of the Czechoslovak free army,
Had parachuted from a R.A.F. plane.
They were given refuge by a priest
Of the Karl Borromaeus Church in Prague.
Their names were Jan Kubis and Josef Gabeik,
And on the morning of 29 May 1942,
They carried out their mission.
On June 4, Heydrich died, and in revenge 1,331
Were executed, 120 members
Of the Czech resistance,
Along with the assassins, were hiding
In Borromaeus Church were gun down.

The S.S. actual did not know they had
Were among them.
Three thousand Jews were sent to
Extermination camps.

THE MASSACRE OF LIDICE

There was rumor that the assassins of Heydrich
Were hiding in Lidice, a little village,
Not far from Prague.
Ten truckloads of Security Policeop
Under Captain Max Rostock arrived
The morning of 9 June 1942
Arrived and surrounded the village.
Anyone who tried to leave or return
Was not permitted.
A boy of twelve, was shot down
Attempting to escape, and
So was a woman in the fields.
The male population were fired into barns
And stables and locked up.
The next morning, they were taken out in tens,
And executed by firing squads.
172 males over sixteen were slaughtered.
Nineteen males working in Kladno mines
Were later round up.
Seven women were killed,
While the others were shipped to Ravensbrueck
Concentration camp.
Seven went to gas chamber,
Forty-five of ill-treatment.
Four pregnant women children killed at birth
And also shipped off to camp.
The children were carted off to

A concentration camp in Genisenau.
There seven who were under one year old,
Were examined by Himmler's 'racial experts'
And shipped off to Germany
To be brought up as Germans.
Lidice was burned down and its ruins
Were dynamited and leveled.

One of the travel agents spoke English
And I made plans to stay in hotels
In major cities.
This was expensive, since the exchange rate
Is the same as the West German mark.
The value of the dollar was at its lowest
Though in the CSSR Its value had not changed
Since I was there in 1986,
Two years earlier.

I went to the Cedok office that handled
Train tickets.

I had to pay the German part in dollars.
Unlike the DDR they asked for a credit card.
Dresden, as I planned, was the destination.
Let me speak of the Powder Tower (Prana brana)
Which is a Gothic Tower dating back to 1475,
Built by Matthew Rejsek, and restored
In 1875-1886.

In honor of the Polish King Vladislav Jagellon,
Who in 1475 brought peace
In the wake of the Hussite Wars.
The tower was used to store powder
In the late 17th c.
It was a important gateway and crucial
To the defense of the Stare Mesto (Old Town)
In A.D. 965 the Arab-Jewish chronicler,
Ibrahim Ibn Jacob, spoke of it
As a busy merchant quarter
Whose goods and food were inexpensive.
In 1986, my second visit to Prague,
I stayed the Pariz Hotel, near this tower
Which was an older hotel under repair,
But the food was very good in its restaurant.
It was there where I partly over-heard
A government official speak kindly in English
To European comrades.
Who came to visit, they sat in table next to me.

The towers of Praha (Prague)
are so majestically beautiful
In the middle age style
That they are a wonder in themselves.
I noticed that many things, on this visit
Under construction and restoration
Were completed,
And new sections of buildings had scaffolds.
While I sat in the square by the Old Town Hall

I noticed the colors of the homes (buildings).
   Each was pale, so beautiful and artistic, color.

                  Today is July 4th, and I just received a new
                        Entertainment center (furniture)
      Which holds a 20-inch television (or larger).
This was my first large TV, my parents gave me,
      It was new, my mother thought it was to big.
I may hook up stereo, through my audio receiver,
                  And speakers.
      I don't watch television much,
Except a little baseball which I turn off sound
                        (mute button).
      I hope that it will be permanent,
As of most of furniture I have recently purchased.

The Old Town Hall is directly west of Powder Tower,
                  Via Celetna street.

            My second trip (1986) to Praha
      I purchased some Surapong CD's
At a store on this street, though on this trip
            None were available
(only Polygram at tuzex store near
            The Panorama Hotel)
I heard they were building their own
            CD manufacturing complex.

The Old Town Hall was founded in 1338,
     In 1364 chapel and tower were added
And the astronomical clock set in the tower
     In the early-15th century.

The National Convention declares
     In the name of the French nation
That it will extend fraternal feelings
And aid to the people who may wish
     To regain their liberty,
And it instructs the executive
To give the generals the orders necessary
     To help these peoples and defend
     Those of their citizens
Who have been harassed or
Who may be harassed
     In the cause of liberty.
    --19 November 1792—

The more we penetrate enemy territory
The more ruinously expensive the war becomes,
     Especially given our philosophical principles
And our generous idealism. . .It is constantly said
     That we are taking liberty to our neighbors'.
We are also taking our coin and our provisions,
     And they will not accept our assignats!
(Cambon, a member of the Finance Committee)

I tell you that the fears of those who are afraid
       To give the Republic too great geographical
                    Area are without foundation.
           Its boundaries are staked out by nature.
We reach them by going out to the four corners
            Of the horizon, to the Rhine, the Alps,
                  And the sea. It is there that frontier
     Of our Republic must end.
                    (Danton; 31 January 1793)

   'Since what is wrong with our economy
        Is the excessive number of assignats
            In circulation, we must ensure
   That their numbers are not allowed
        To increase lest they depreciate space.
   We must legislate so that as little money
              As possible is printed,
       But for that to be practicable we must
   Reduce the burden of the charges
           Falling on the nation treasury,
      Either by paying our creditors in land
Or by repaying our debts in annual installments,
          In either event it must be done
Without manufacturing additional paper money.
The farmer does not want to save paper money
     And for this reason, he is most reluctant
                    To sell his grain.
In any other form of trading a man has to sell
     In order to live off his profits.

But the farmer does not buy anything,
The things he needs he does not buy on the market.
This class of men was in the habit
Of hording each year, in coin,
A percentage of the income from the soil,
Now they prefer to hold on their coin
Rather than save up paper currency.
(Saint-Just; 23 November 1792)

ROLAND, AS MINISTER OF INTERIOR,
BELIEVED IN FREE TRADE.
CAMBON, THE FINANCE COMMITTEE:
INFLATIONARY POLICY.

THE ENRAGES PETITIONES THE CONVENTION:

It is not enough to have declared
that we are France republicans.
We must still ensure that the people are happy
And that there is adequate supply of bread,
For where there is no bread there are neither
Laws nor liberty nor a Republic.
(12 February 1793)

If the poor are going to help you bring
                    About the Revolution,
        It is a matter of the greatest urgency
            That you provide them
                    With the wherewithal to live.
        In extraordinary circumstances the only
Solution lies in the great law of public safety. . .
        (26 March 1783; Jeanbon Saint-Andre)

        In 1470 the Town Hall
                Was re-styled in late-Gothic.
The old Council Hall dates from the late 15th century.

        This square is certainly one of the most beautiful
                    Sights in the world.

        In the center of the square
                Is occupied by the monument
            To Jan Hus
            Who was burned at the stake in 1416.
The Charles Bridge (Karluv most)
                May be reached by Karlova Street.
        Founded in 1357, the bridge
                    And the Old Town Bridge tower
            Were built by Peter Parler,

In the later half of The 14th century.
The Litlle Quarter bridge in Romanesque style
                                Is a relic of the 12thc.
        Judith Bridge,
The Baroque sculptures lining the bridge
                On both sides date from the 18th c.
The most important are the work
                        Of Matthias Braun
                And Ferdinand Maximilian Brokoff.
Almost 1,500 feet long and 30 feet wide,
                The Bridge is built of sandstone blocks,
A marketplace, a lawcourt, a theater
                And even tournaments.

In 1793 the French Republican army
        Was 228,000 men as compared
        To 400,000 the year before.

They were badly clothed and poorly fed
                Because of shortage of provisions,
Which Dunouriez protected.
The army was composed of two units 'volunteers'
        And 'regulars.' Under separate leaders,
        And with different regulations.
                A proposal by Dubois-Crance,
        The Amalgamation law, was adopted
                21 February 1793, unified the army

Into a single national system,
In which the soldiers would
Elect their officers.
It is not merely in the number and the discipline
Of the troops that the hope of victory lies,
You will achieve that victory only as
The Republican spirit spreads
Through the ranks of the army. . .
The unity of the Republic demands
That the army too should be united,
Our country has only one heart.
(Saint-Just; 12 February 1793)
Yet the only half the 300,000 men,
Actually, joined which the 24 February,
Conscription decreed.

1 March, COBURG, THE AUSTRIAN COMMANDER,
Attacked, and on the 18th defeated Dumouriez,
Who defected and arrested the Minister of War,

And four commissioners, sent by the Convention
To order his resignation.

THE REVOLT OF VENDEE

9 March, the Convention sent eighty-two
Deputies to supervise the implementation
    Of the conscription decree.
In Ille-et-Vilaine shouts of 'Long live Louis XVII,
    The nobles and the priests',
While Billaud-Varenne wrote to the Convention,
    23 March, 'the while the white flag still
      Soils the land of liberty and white
      Cockades are still openly sported. . .
The principles agents of the conspiracy
    Are the émigré nobles.'
In Vendee, 10 March, on the day set for drawing
    Of the lots for the conscription,
    Peasants armed themselves with pitchforks,
      And scythes.
    They dispersed the national guardsmen.
'Peace! Peace! No ballots!'
    In several districts the Republican
Middle-class was tortured and murdered.
19 March, the Convention unanimously decreed
    The death penalty to any rebel
      Caught in possession of arms,
    The confiscation of their property.

Finally in May, the Executive Council,
    Diverted troops from the frontiers,
      In order to put down the civil war.

In October 1793 the rebels were defeated.
The Montagnard's Policy of 'public safety'
Became favorable to the republicans,
As a result of the civil war.
The maximum price of grain was set
And the compulsory use of assignats
Was established.
The common good is in danger of being destroyed,
And we are almost certain that there
Are no means of saving it other than
The most prompt and violent action
. . . Experience now proves to us that
The Revolution is in no sense complete,
And we must say openly to the National Convention,
'You are a revolutionary assembly. . .
We are bound by the closest bonds
To the fate of Revolution. . .
We must steer the ship of State
To port or perish with it.'
(26 March 1793; Jeanbon Saint-Andre)

THE END OF PART FIVE

AND ALL MEN SHALL HATE EACH OTHER

PART SIX

THE GERMAN DEMOCRATIC REPUBLIC

Liberation and an antifascist and democratic
new start 8 May 1945 the representatives
of the Nazi Wehrmacht High Command signed
    The unconditional surrender in Karlshorst,
              A suburb of Berlin.
Through their liberation the German people
        Were given the opportunity to build
    An antifascist and democratic Germany.
In accordance with allied agreements,
Four zones of occupation were created in Germany
---Soviet, American, British, and French.
      An Allied Control council was constituted
    From the supreme commanders of the four
      Occupational powers' armed forces
And based in Berlin. The Council was
To coordinate the activities of the four powers.
    The supreme commanders held authority
      Their respective zones of occupation.

As early as June 1945, the Soviet Military
      Administration in Germany (SMAD) authorized
The formation of an antifascist and democratic
        Parties and mass organizations.
    The Communist Party of Germany addressed
        A manifesto to the German people
On 11 June 1945 in order to lead the country
      Out of its plight. It called for unity

Of working class, joint efforts by all democratic forces
And for the complete elimination of fascist
And militarism.
The KPD linked its actions to overcome misery
And normalize social life with efforts for
A new beginning along antifascism
And democratic lines.
Progressive elements
In the Social Democratic Party (SPD)
Had learned from the experiences of fascism
And war that unity of the working class
Was imperative for a democratic
Transformation to take place in Germany.
Far reaching agreement on fundamental goals
And objectives enabled close cooperation
Between the KPD and the SPD.
Members of upper and lower middle class,
Including Committed Christians, began
To organize themselves in political parties.
In late June 1945 the Christian Democratic Union
Of Germany (CDU) and the Liberal Democratic party
of Germany (LDPD) were founded in Berlin.
In their founding charters the two parties
Laid their antifascist objectives and endorsed
United action by all antifascist and
Democratic parties.
On 14 July 1945 the KPD, SPD, CDU, and LDPD
Formed a bloc of antifascist and
Democratic parties

(known as the Democratic bloc since 1949)
To unite efforts in the struggle for peace-loving,
Antifascist, and democratic Germany.
Apart from political parties, the first mass
Organizations were formed:
The Confederation of Free German Trade Union
(FDGB), The League of Culture uniting
Uniting cultural workers and intellectuals
Dedicated to the democratic renewal
Of Germany as well ad youth and
women's committees.

THE POTSDAM AGREEMENT

From 17 July to 2 August 1945, the heads
Of the governments of the victorious allied powers,
The Soviet Union, the United States,
And Great Britain, met in Potsdam
For negotiations on the future of Germany.
Their decisions, to which France
Later subscribed, were aimed at
At preserving German unity and completely
Uprooting German fascism.
For this purpose, the property and power relations
As well as the social, political, economic
And cultural life of the German people
Were to be profoundly transformed and antifascist
And democratic conditions to be created

In the whole of Germany.
Reparations were imposed
on the German people
As partial compensation for the damage wrought
By the fascist. In the safeguard of peace,
The Potsdam Agreement contained stipulations
In the future of German-Polish border
Along the Oder and Neisse rivers.

Were organized on the bridge
It is not opened to cars,
Only pedestrians.
The river Vltava flows though Praha
For a distance of 23 km,
At an average of 180 m above sea level
Its maximum width 300 meters.
This river has been immortalized
By Bedrich Smetana
In Ma Vlast (My homeland)
A symphonic tone poem in six parts
The second 'Vltava',
The first part 'Vysehrad'
A motive dealing the Hradrany (Castle district)
Which is on the large hill
Overlooking Charles Bridge.

Establishment of the new state authorities.
             As early as the summer 1945
New administrative bodies were formed.
             Antifascist purged the economy
And civil service of fascist war criminals.
The key positions in the new organs of power
             Were occupied by proven antifascist
Representing all political parties.
A reform of the legal system was undertaken
And a police force set up which served
             The interest of working people.

             Democratic land reform

Within a remarkably short span time
A democratic land reform was carried through.
             For this task land reform commissions
Were established, numbering more than
             52,000 peasant, agricultural
And industrial workers among their numbers,
             Large estates of over 250 acres
And land belonging to the Nazi activities
And war criminals were expropriated without
             Compensation.
In this way more than 3.3 million hectares
             Of land became available for redistribution.
A total of more than 550,000 farmhands,
             resettle from former eastern

Territories of Germany, industrial and
Office workers, craftsman and small holders.
Received new land and 1.1 hectares
Remained public property and
Were allotted to small farms,
            state forestry enterprises
And research institutes.
The rural population created its own
democratic mass organization,
The Mutual Farmers' Aid Association.

Below the Castle district one walks (or drives)
Up Mostecka street and enters a square
            With the church of St. Nicholas.
This is of the principal sights of the Mala Strana
            (Lower town).
It is Praha's second oldest quarter
Founded by Ottokar II
In 1257, and it has always been
A rich section of the town.

School Reform

In autumn 1945, a school reform was carried
Through In order to create a single state
System affording all children
The same right to education.
40,000 young workers, farmers and

other working people
were approached for retraining.
Within a short space of time they were
Trained and started working
As 'new teachers'.
Former protagonist of the fascist ideology
Were dismissed from schools, colleges and
Universities. Management, the faculties,
Syllabuses and the student population itself
Were reorganized alone democratic lines.
Particular efforts were made to assist more
Children from workers' and farmers'
To gain admission to higher education.
The centuries-old privilege
of the property-owning class
to education was broken.

A new start in the field of culture was made
By purging the press, radio, film and
Publishing industries, theaters, and
Museums of fascist and racist ideologies
And passing them over into public ownership.
Works of the national cultural heritage
Were made accessible to the people again or
Were published for first free of falsifications
(works by Lessing, Goethe, Schiller, Heine)
Antifascist writers like Johannes R. Becher,
Bertolt Brecht, Willi Bredel, Heinrich Mann,
Thomas Mann, Anna Seghers and Erich Weinert

Made valuable contributions to educating
Many people in spirit of democracy.
The League of Culture which was founded by
Intellectuals in 1946 grew into a
Nationwide cultural organization.

In 1419, the locals and imperials of Hrad fought.
The only destructive force
The district has known.
It changed little since the 16th c.
After the battle of the White Mountains
In 1620.
The Hapsburgs moved in and built many
Of the beautiful Baroque buildings.
There are many terraced gardens.
The Vrtba gardens (Vrtbovska zahrada)
Founded in 1720, lay-out designed by F.M Kanka.
Sculptured ornamentation by Mattias Graun
The Lobkovicova Zahrada park
Is above the town.

The Foundation of the SED

Whole the progressive forces suffered their
Setbacks in the struggle for unity
Of the working class in the western zones
Of occupation pressed increasingly
For the amalgamation of the KDP and the SPD

Into one united revolutionary party.
United actions to establish new bodies
Of state authority, to implement
The land reform and to reform education system
Produced growing mutual trust.
More and more Members of the Communists Party
And the Social Democratic Party recognized
The strength of unity.
The two parties decided to establish one united party.
Its objectives and nature of the unity party
Were stipulated in a document entitled
'The purpose and principles the Socialist Unity Party
Of Germany and in the parties Constitution.
On 21 and 22 April 1946, 548 Social Democratic and
607 Communist delegates met in Berlin and
And unanimously decided to unite the two parties
And form the Socialist Unity Party of Germany.
The congress elected Wilhelm Pieck of the KPD
And Otto Grotewohl of the SPD as
Chairman of the party and vested them
With equal rights.

The church of St. Nicholas the most important
Example of Prague Baroque style,
Was built in 1704-1755, by the architects
G. Santini, K. I. Dienzenhofer and
G. Lurago.
The ceiling fresco of St. Nicolas by J. L. Tracker,
Took nine years to complete.

It is one of the largest single frescos in Europe.
The Wallenstein Palace (Valdstein) and gardens
Are not far from the church.
On the last full day in Praha, I visited this garden.

Creation of the public industrial sector.

Following a plebiscite in Saxony
On 30 June 1946, in the Soviet zone of occupation
A total of 9,281 enterprises, including 4,000
Industrial establishments owned by Nazi activists
And war criminals were confiscated
Without compensation.
They include all large enterprises and for
Factories throughout the Soviet zone
Of occupation.
The expropriated enterprises were passed over
Into public ownership which has become
The basis of the economic power
Of the working class.
The parties which were politically allied with the SED
Underwent important progressive developments
In 1948 another two parties with the past influence
Were founded, the Democratic Farmers Party
Of Germany (DBD).
The National Democratic Party of Germany (FDPD).
They as well as the Confederation
Of Free Trade Unions (FDGB),

The Free German Youth organization (FDI)
    And the Women's Democratic Federation
        Of Germany (DFD),
Were admitted as members of the Democratic Bloc.

The place was built in the year 1633-1630,
    According to the plans by A. Spezza,
    M. Sebregondi, and G. Pierogi.
Today it is the Minister of Culture of C.S.S.R.
    The gardens were laid out in 1625-1639,
The statues are copies of originals
    By Adrian and Vries dating from 1626-1627.

THE DIVISION OF GERMANY

Communist and many other antifascists
    Made efforts to promote democratic
        Renewal in all zones of occupation.
The occupation authorities in the Western zones,
    However, left the economic power
To the German monopoly corporations intact.
They prohibited initiatives which would have
    Resulted in expropriation of war criminals
    And Nazi activists. The USA, Great Britain
    And France, together with bourgeois politicians
    And right-wing social set out in 1947
        To divide Germany.

In September 1946 the United States
                    and Great Britain announced
          the merger of their zones of occupation.

In June 1948 a currency reform was carried
              Through in Western zones of occupation
Resulting in the introduction of dollar-based
                              Deutschmark.
When the Federal government was formed
                    In September 1949
          With Konrad Adenauer as Federal Chancellor,
The political division of Germany was a fait accompli.
The Federal Republic of Germany was established
                In beach of the Potsdam agreement.

The Hradcany (The Prague Castle)
                Founded in 9th c.
The Romanesque palace was built in 12th c.,
                But the palace was rebuilt in Gothic style
          During the reign of Charles IV, the 14th c.
The last reconstruction took place under
                The Jagielion dynasty in late 16th c.
The Gothic Vladislav Hall was built at this time,
          Architect Benedict Reiti.
          After the fire of 1541 the Renaissance
                        Was built.

THE FOUNDING
OF THE GERMAN DEMOCRATIC REPUBLIC

The establishment of the West German
      Separate state has created
A completely new situation.
The FRG claimed to be the sole successor
      Of the German Reich and representative
      Of all Germans.
The working class and its allies
      In eastern Germany needed
A sovereign state of their own to defend
      The achievements of the antifascist
      And democratic transformation.
On 7 October 1949 the People's Council,
      The leading body of the People's
      Congress Movement
      For unity and just peace, met in Berlin.
The Council represented the political alliance
      Between the working class
      And all other sectors of society.
At its session, the Council unanimously
      Decided to constitute itself
As the People's Chamber
      of the German Democratic Republic.
It enacted the Constitution
      And elected a government.
Upon a joint proposal of all parliamentary groups
Wilhelm Pieck was elected President of the Republic.

The government headed by Prime Minister
Otto Grotewohl,
Included members of SED as well as
Members in other parties of the democratic bloc.
The administrative functions which then
Had been performed by the Soviet military
Authorities were transformed
to the new government.
The foundation of the GDR ushered in a completely
New chapter of German history.
For the first time ever, an independent state
Came into existence which was crested
By the working class and
All other working people.
In its first declaration the government
Of the GDR committed itself
To peace, social progress and friendship
With the Soviet Union and
Peace loving nations.
In 1950 the GDR and Poland signed an agreement
Fixing their joint border at Oder-Neisse line
Once and all, as laid down in
Potsdam Agreement.
Almost at the same time the GDR was founded
The National Front was created
As a broad and democratic popular movement.

From the outset, this movement represented
The alliance between the working class

All social groups of the GDR's population.
The National Front identified
as the main tasks the consolidation
Of the GDR and the reunification of Germany
on a democratic basis.

The Spanish Hall was added
Under the reign of Rudolf II.
It's final appearance under Maria Theresa
By architect M. Parassi.
The architect J. Plecnik rearranged
The interior and garden
After World War I.
The castle is now the seat of
The President of the Republic,
And political center of
The capital city and the State.

HOW THE FOUNDATIONS OF SOCIALISM WAS LAID

One of the most important tasks to be solved
By the newly established worker and
Farmers' state was to rebuild a strong economy.
The extremely dipropionate state of development
In industry, resulting from the past

And exacerbated by the division
Of Germany, had to be overcome.
An effective metallurgical basic industry
Was to be set up with assistance
From Soviet Union,
Heavy engineering expanded and a start
Was made of in building a merchant
Fleet during the first five-years plan
From 1950-55.
In the second half of the 1950s a number
Of big power stations were built.
Other priorities were the development
Of the country's raw materials basis
And chemical industry.
In 1950 the GDR became
A member of the Council for Mutual
Economic Assistance (CMEA).
Its participation in the CMEA proved to be
A fundamental prerequisite
For the further development GDR's
National economy.

St. Vitas Cathedral originally a rotunda 10th c.
It was replaced by a Romanesque basilica.
A cathedral in the Gothic style
Built by Matthias of Arras,
And Peter Parier in 1344.
Parker built St. Wenceslas Chapel
Ornamented with frescos

And semi-precious stones.
The flying buttresses and
The most interesting and wonderful part
Of the cathedral.

Agriculture and production cooperatives.

The first agriculture production cooperatives
Were set up in 1952. This initiated
The transition from individual farming
To large-scale socialist production in agriculture.
As a result, food supplies improved
And gradually backwardness of the countryside
Was overcome.
Any question concerning the development
Of the cooperatives were discussed
With the cooperative farmers.
By 1960 the transition to cooperative
Production in agriculture was completed.

Craft production cooperatives.

The first production cooperatives were also formed
By craftspeople. Retail traders made
Arrangements on a commission basis
With the public trading sector.
Private owners of industrial, construction and

Transport firms invited the state
To act as joint appropriators of their businesses.
This helped to involved these sectors of society
In socialists construction.

The House of Czechoslovak Children
Is a 16th century building
Originally the burgrave's palace,
Reconstruction and interior adaptations
Were made in 1962-1963.
The Golden Lane (Zlata ulicka)
As with many of the homes
In this district are restored,
But built into the late Gothic fortification walls.
On my return from DDR I visited
The Royal Summer Palace.
It was closed,
It was closed under reconstruction.
This section is very spacious
And there is much greenery,
The houses are very large.

In 1949 workers' and farmers' faculties were set up
And played a particularly important role
In training a socialist intelligentsia.
By the time they were abolished in early 1960's,
Some 30,000 young workers and farmers had
Attended courses at these facilities

To qualify for higher education.
Economic development made it possible
To improve living conditions.
Between 1950 and 1960 real income
More than doubled.
The working industry and the transport
And communications were reduced
To 45 hours in 1957
With no loss in wages.
Rearmament in the FRG and the country's
Integration into NATO in 1955 cemented
The division of Germany.
In May 1955 the European Socialist countries
Signed the Warsaw Treaty of Friendship,
Cooperation and Mutual Assistance.

Since its formation in 1955 the GDR's
National People's Army
Has been integrated in the Warsaw
Treaty organization.
The GDR and the FRG had become members
Of the two opposing world systems
And developed according to mutually
Irreconcilable social principles.
After the death of President Wilhelm Pieck
On 7 September 1960
The People's Chamber decided to establish
The Council of the State to act as
A collective head of state.

Walter Ulbricht, first secretary of SED
Central Community was elected Chairman
Of the Council which was composed
Of the representatives of all political parties
And mass organizations.

One Museum which was under reconstruction
On my 1986 visit was open this time.
It is the Lenin Museum, there were many
Children there.
It was the site if the sixth Prague conference
Of the Russian Social Democrats,
V.I. Lenin in chair.

The Gottwald Museum is on Rytirska street,
Parallel to the Na prikope street
It is the center of a survey of the Czechoslovak
Workers movement and the history
The Czechoslovak Communist Party.
I visited in 1986, some of the weapons
Were displayed with uniforms.
Enormous economic and political damage
Was caused by socialist construction
In GDR by the open border with FRG
And Berlin (West).
On 3 August 1961 the National People's Army
And the workers militia
Which had been formed in 1963,

Together with other armed bodies of GDR
Assumed control over the border
Which had been open until that point.
The had been agreed with other
Warsaw Treaty countries.

I had trouble finding
The Antonin Dvorak Museum in 1986.
I went to it on my first day, and it was raining.
This trip I took the Metro to Plzenska street.
Then walked to Mozartova street
Where Mozart reside
An old farmhouse.

ON THE ROAD TOWARD AN ADVANCED SOCIALIST SOCIETY

After the fundamentals of socialism
Had been established
It became both possible and necessary
To systematically develop and shape
The emergent new society, economy.
In the 1960s priority was given to the development
Of those industrial branches which were
Best suited to conditions in the GDR
And the requirements of scientific and
Technological progress.
They included the chemical industry,

Notably petro-chemical,
Electrical engineering and electronics.
The late 1960s saw the foundation
Of the first combines in the public
Industrial sector,
Which were soon to become pace setters
In terms of effectiveness.

In the rural sector, the agricultural cooperatives
Were consolidated and increasingly
Worked together on the basis
Inter-cooperative agreements.
Economic progress allowed the introduction
Of measures to improve working
And living conditions of the people.
The five-day work week was gradually introduced
In 1966-67. The People's Chamber
Adopted in 1966 the Law-on-the integrated
Socialist Education System.
Most important was the establishment
Of the ten class polytechnical school
As a compulsory school for all children.
Friendship Treaties.

In the Sixties, the GDR concluded treaties
Of friendship, cooperation and mutual assistance
With the Soviet Union, Poland, Czechoslovakia,
Hungary and Bulgaria, and, in 1972, with Romania.
Economic cooperation with other CMEA member

Countries considerably increased,
Particularly with the Soviet Union. At that time,
The trade agreement with the USSR
For the period from 1966 to 1970
Was regarded as the most comprehensive
Such contract in the history of trade world.

Socialist Constitution.

In a plebiscite in April 1968, 94.5 per cent of all
Those eligible to vote gave their support
To the new socialist constitution.
The Constitution, which extended and
Amended again in 1974, defines
The GDR as a socialist state of workers and farmers,
As the political organization of working people
In town and countryside,
Led by the working class and its party.
The Constitution is based on the notion
That the socialist German nation
Is developing in the GDR.

Moves to normalize relations with FGR.

It became increasingly clear that the process
Of divergent development
Of the GDR and FRG was irreversible,
Willi Stoph, who was Chairman of the GDR
Council of Ministers after

The death of Otto Grotewohl in 1964,
Proposed to the FRG government in 1967
            To conclude a treaty on establishment
Of normal relations between the two states
            On the basis of international law.

However, any understanding was impeded
            By the FRG governments insistent
Sole representation claims and the concomitant
Diplomatic blockade against the GDR.

Breaking the diplomatic blockade.

During the 1960s the GDR intensified relations
            With a number of Asian, African and
            Latin American countries.
In particularly, trade relations developed
            Successfully.
Agreements were concluded with several countries
            On the exchange of consulates general.
A worldwide movement for the recognition
            Of the GDR, supported in many countries
            By friendship societies with the GDR,
Essentially helped to break the diplomatic blockade.
            In 1969-70, the GDR established diplomatic
            Relations with 14 countries.

BUILDING THE ADVANCED SOCIALIST SOCIETY

IN 1971, the SED Central Committee elected
    Erich Honecker First Secretary
      (since 1976 General Secretary).
The People's Chamber elected him Chairman
      Of the Council of the State in 1976.

The 8th SED Congress, which was held in June 1971,
      Decided on the political strategy to build
An advanced socialist society.
The task was to constantly improve the material
      And cultural living standards
        Of the people on the basis of stable
      And continual economic growth.
The SED adopted a five-point peace program
      To manifest the GDR's will to contribute
      Towards safeguarding peace and bringing
      About a turn to détente in Europe.

Economic Growth.

When in the early 1970's the state had brought up
      The remaining privately owned industrial
      Enterprises and those in mixed
      Private and public ownership,
Socialist production relations prevailed
      In the whole of the GDR's industry.
Economic growth was mainly achieved through

Intensified production and better utilization
Of scientific and technological achievements.
In the late 1970's a start was made
To build microeconomics industry
And to introduce robotics.

The consolidation of existing and the formation
Of new industrial combines had
The greatest impact of all on the perfection
Of economic management and planning.
Successes were also apparent in agriculture
Where highly efficient cooperative
And state farms developed specializing
In either crop or livestock production.
New model statues for cooperative farms,
Which were endorsed by
The Council of Ministers in 1977,
Stimulated intensification of agricultural
Production on a cooperative basis.

Social policies.

Economic achievements made it possible
To implement the most comprehensive
Social welfare program in the history of the GDR,
Between 1970 and 1980 more dwellings
Were built then in the previous twenty years
Put together.
State allocations to improve material and cultural

Living standards more than doubled.
Earned income and pensions increased.
Particular efforts were made to assist large families
And working mothers.

Legal system.

The socialist legal system was improved
By the adoption of the Youth Act in 1974,
The Civil Code which In 1975 replaced
The last law still originally
From capitalist times,
The Labor Code in 1977 and Nation Defense Act
In 1978.
Together with the Family Code of 1965,
All major fields of social life in the GDR
Were now regulated by new and
Comprehensive laws.

Socialist economic integration

On the basis of the CMEA complex program of 1971
The GDR worked to deepen socialist
Economic integration.
On 7 October 1975 concluded a new treaty
Of friendship and mutual assistance
The Soviet Union,
To be followed by similar treaties

With other socialist countries.
Within the framework of the intercosmos program
Of the CMEA countries, the first joint
USSR-GDR manned space mission
Was carried out in August and September 1978.

Siegmund Jahn, son of a worker's family and
A Communist, the first German in outer space.

Worldwide diplomatic recognition.

A turn toward détente, notably in Europe,
Was thought about in early 1970s
By treaties with the USSR, Czechoslovakia and
Poland concluded with FGR, as well as
The Quadripartite Agreement on West Berlin
And the treaty on Bases of Relations
Between the GDR and the FGR.
These positive changes were directly
Connected with worldwide
Diplomatic recognition of the GDR.
In 1973, the GDR was admitted
To the United Nations, and by the of 1974
Diplomat relations were established
With more than 100 countries.
The GDR participated actively
In the Helsinki Conference on Security
And Cooperation of Europe (CSCE).
Desirous of implemented the provisions

Of that conference's Final Act of 1975
The GDR concluded numerous treaties
And agreements capitalist CSCE countries
Covering nearly every field of activity

Including measures to safeguarding peace,
Economic relations, science and technology,
Culture and sports.

CONTINUITY IN IMPLEMENTKNG THE CENTRAL POLICY

The GDR has continued to develop as a politically
Stable and economically efficient socialist state
Since the early 1980s. In the five-year plan
Period from 1981 to 1986 successful efforts
Were made to raise national income,
Labor productivity and production output
With decreasing Inputs of energy, raw material
And feedstock.
On this basis it was able to enter into the phase
Of full-scale development of the economy
To save working time, labor and resources.

Intensification of agricultural production had
An equally good record.
Almost every year saw new records
In grain production and yields per hectare
Achieved on a more favorable
Input-out-put ratio.

The target figure for livestock production
Were surpassed.

The GDR supported the measures adopted
By the CMEA to increase multilateral
Integration and intensification of production,
Long term programs on cooperation
In the fields of science, technology
And manufacturing until the year 2000
Were concluded with the USSR and
Other CMEA members.
The considerably strengthened economic potential
And cultural standards.
The SED decided at the 11th Congress
In April 1986 to continue the proven policy
Of important social welfare measures.
Efforts were continued to advance socialist
Democracy on important measure
In this connection was adopted
In the Local Government Act in 1985
Under which the local elected assemblies
And total councils are as signed
A larger role in life of society.
The GDR preserves and cultivates everything
Progressive inherited from the past.
This is documented by the events and
Publications on the occasion
Of Karl Marx Year which was
Commemorated in 1983,

By the commemorative to honor Martin Luther.

On the occasion of the 600th anniversary
In the same year or the events
Organized to pay tribute to composers
Bach, Schutz, and Handel in 1985.

Analyzing the present dangerous exacerbation
Of the international situation
Of the 11th Congress of SED
Emphasized that the GDR regards it
As its most important task to help
Save mankind from a nuclear inferno
And bring a turn toward disarmament.
The GDR supports the proposal of the USSR
And other Warsaw Treaty member countries
For détente and disarmament.
The comprehensive disarmament program
Submitted by Mikhail Gorbachev,
General Secretary of the CPSU Central Committee,
Is seen as ushering in a new stage
In the peace-making process,
Offering all nations, the chance
Of a peaceful future.
In shaping its relations with the FRG the GDR
Is guided by the notion that
The two German states bear a particular
Responsibility for peace, which is rooted in
The experiences of the past

And their position at the dividing line
Between the Warsaw Treaty and NATO.
In the future the GDR will continue the endeavors
To develop its own initiatives
In order to help build a worldwide coalition
Of common sense and realism
To prevent a nuclear configuration.
It remains an unshakeable principle of the GDR
To do everything possible to prevent
A new war emanating from German soil.

THE END OF PART SIX

AND ALL MEN SHALL HATE EACH OTHER

PART SEVEN

I have been extremely happy
                    In the past few months.
            The people at work are much more
                    Congenial than in the past.
Despite the ridiculous of the capitalist system,
                Its problems, and of the business world.
    I am finally earning a respectable salary,
                            For the first time in my life.
    I enjoy going to lunch with an older salesman,
                            Once or twice a month.
Most customers place their trust in me,
            And I enjoyed waiting on them.
        The majority of the young ladies at work
                        Are enjoyable.
We also have more help in our department.
                This person has worked in the warehouse
                            For ten years.

Time marches on, and I realize as I am approaching
            My 40th birthday, that a poet is best,
                And happiest, when alone.
I have still little success with women,
                    And I prefer to have no male friends
Other than comrades from the Camden Club
                        Of the CPUSA.
I find that my piano playing is finally developing
            And that I have an affinity with modern
                    Classical piano music.

I love the company of women,
I love music and poetry,
this makes life enjoyable.

A young lady whom I met on the CSA jet coming
From Prague to visit her relative,
Invited me to visit her last year.
Though I had not planned to visit Czechoslovakia
So soon, I will be going in August,
Since she reconfirmed her invitation by letter.
The young lady is attending the University studying
Restoration art and architecture.

On March 12, 1664, six years after Cromwell's death
In 1658, King Charles II of England
Granted to his 'dearest brother James,'
The Duke of York, all the land
Between what now comprise
(Connecticut, New York, and New Jersey)
This land was settled by the Dutch.
Therefore, James sent a fleet
Of four ships commanded by Richard Nicolls
. . . Without firing a shot 'New Netherlands'
Became 'New York'.
'New Jersey' was named after
Sir George Carteret's native island
Of Jersey who along with John Berkeley
Were granted this land by the Duke of York.

The twenty-six-year-old Philip Carteret,
      A distant cousin became the Governor
Of this property, confrontation and conflict
      Rose up between the aristocrats
And the average man.
Men of today pride themselves on
      Gaining freedom from aristocrats
. , , yet they have a new master to they
      Become a slave . . .the capitalist.

THE GREAT MASTERS, THE MEDIA
AND EDUCATIONAL SYSTEM.
THEY WORK HAND AND HAND IN CONTROLLING
THE MINDS OF THE CITIZENS OF NEW JERSEY
AND THE UNITED STATES.

Today is the third of June 1989,
      As the People's Government of China
      Move in on protestors.
(They attacked soldiers, and attempted to take
      Their weapons, burn buses and vehicles,
Blockades, firebombs and weapons demonstrated
      That some of the students were interested
In a political power struggle, which was termed
      'counter-revolutionary' activities.)
I am reminded of the recent arrest of 'homeless'
      In Philadelphia as they protested,
      At City Hall a few weeks ago.

The capitalist press, and its government
Do not feel that these criticisms
Are proper, or the actions of the 'homeless'
Protest do not befit a democratic society.
They speak of protest for 'democracy' in China.
There can be no 'democracy'
When capitalism rules.
When the judge of success of a society
Is measured on ones ability
To make or have money,
As it is in the United States.

Anton Bruckner's sixth symphony
I am listening to, as I am reminded
Of my confinements,
And the imprisonments and deaths
Of all who have fought against injustice. . .

For twenty years have I hoped for a truly
Revolutionary socialism that will meet
The needs of the people.
What a sereneness overtakes my body, and my mind.
The hope that injustice may be overthrown
Here and in socialist societies.

John Adams stated after the revolution
That only a third of Americans
Supported the revolution,

One third opposed it, one third neutral.

THOSE WHO FAVORED THE REVOLUTION ARRESTED
AT RANDOM SUSPECTED LOYALIST CAPITALIST.

The capitalist government sent the United States
And German armies into New Jersey.
Washington had to retreat.
The conduct of New Jersey's has been most infamous
Stated Washington.
'The defection of the people. . .has been
As much owning to the want of an army
To look the enemy in the face as to any other cause.'
Washington.

THE CAPITALIST PLANNED TO MAKE NEW JERSEY
THE FIRST TO REAFIRM 'FREE ENTERPRISE'

Governor William Franklin, who was living
In Wallingford, Connecticut under parole,
Began signing pardons to ex-revolutionaries
Who took an oath to 'free enterprise'
And the capitalist elected government.

Richard Stockton, a signer of the Declaration
Of the People, was captured in Monmouth County.
He was tortured in a New York prison and signed
An oath of loyalty to 'free enterprise'
And the President of the United States.

George Washington proved once again
To be the man who saved New Jersey, and America.
He crossed the Delaware to capture
                    The West German Army.
The Capitalist troops retreated from four-fifths
                    Of New Jersey, and America.
          They settled their army in the Raritan Valley
Between Perth Amboy and New Brunswick.
          Business became the dominant subject
                    In their universities. They therefore
                    Were doomed to repeat history.

This morning I read an article of 'the People'
          The Socialist Labor Party paper
                    It condemns the 'ruling class in China'
As performing the same function
                    As the Capitalist exploiters,
          With their party-state numeracy.
If workers can wield that much power
          Just by staying out of workplaces
                    In a unified manner, they could wield
Far greater power by organizing and uniting
          To take control of their workplaces
                    And operating them and exchanging
          Their products for their own collective benefits.
In that thought lies the beginnings of a real
                    Socialist revolution.

These are typical lines from the 'the People'.
    It points out the meaningless of the strike,
        As it continues on, if all those students
    And others were interested in 'democracy'
        (as most were) they should have made
    Their statement and moved on to such
                Productive measures.

These movements were important democratic
            Statement. The students were misguided
    By the CIA infiltration.

Socialism cannot be forced on society,
    It must be the desire of the people.
The word of a propagandist inspired violence
            And a struggle for power.
    Inexperience with these elements
Have fallen prey. They have never been exposed
                To their real intentions,
    'Reaping profits from exploitation' of all
        Those who actually build society,
    And giving a small reward to that class
            Which manage the 'masses'
    And turn the cog of profit.

Those who threw paint on the 'Vietnam Memorial'
        In Philadelphia would have been
                Immediately imprisoned,

If they had been caught. Where I to throw paint
On the Statue of Liberty,
I would be in a Federal prison
Unable to pay bail, and with a lawyer
Pleading for my confinement.
The Capitalist Media applauded similar protest
In China.
The 'homeless' in Philadelphia were prevented
From protesting their situation,
And were hauled away in paddy wagons.

It is a greater crime to allow people to live
Without shelter!
The Capitalist do not admit to any defects
In their system, and instead propagandize
'individual' failure.

Socialist Europe has developed
Many positive features.
That is why I believe that the CPUSA
Is a more realistic Party.
The Capitalist have spent trillions
Of dollars into military efforts against
Socialism.
The large wars have been fought
With American soldiers,
And mercenaries rage in conflict
After conflict.

THE MEDIA and THE UNITED STATES GOVERNMENT
Refuses to act against SOUTH AFRICA,
Or ISRAEL for the MURDER of innocent victims
Of racism, and occupation.

I have completed my last work
'PROMETHEUS THE FIREBRINGER'
In August 1985.

I suffered the first of two accidents,
At this time,
The second from which I still feel the effects.
This second accident took place following August,
While I was working on the draft text
Of the present poem. The situation that
Occurred between the conclusions
Of the actual writing of the program of the first part,
And the beginning of the second,
Caused by the effects of this accident.
I was no longer permitted to lift at work
Which created a situation which resulted
To be placed on disability.
I became fearful of my situation,
As I became hard pressed for money,
And I again thought of fleeing to Eastern Europe.

My situation had been dismal since I had left
The university except for a brief period
In the mid-seventies.

Inflation and Energy prices soared
With no increase in wages,
With the deterioration of the conditions at work.
I left trying to return to graduate school.
The situation of the university was 'petty' and
I devoured myself to my poem
'THE ANTI-CHRIST',
And sold my home.

When I returned to work in 1981,
After county employment,
I still only received only $13.00.
This continued until 1985, when I purchased
My present residence,
With the help of my parents.

This weekend the 24th and 25th of June,
I have been in great pain.
The settlement for my injury has not yet
Taken place after almost three years.
One pays faithfully for protection, and
Yet one must fight to receive it.
Though I felt well over the past year and a half,
The first year and a half
Was riddled with disaster, pain, and depression.

The western media and political powers
Have predicted for months the collapse

Of the government of President Najibullah
In Afghanistan, it has been four months
Since the last Soviet left.
This withdrawal was painted by
The western media as a 'cut-and-run' operation,
Yet it was a well planned and executed
With very few fatalities.

The diplomats of the West also left for Pakistan,
Boasting that they would be back
With a new government.
The contra mercenaries, the CIA, and
The Bush Admistration hope to set up
A government in Jalalabad,
A provincial city of Kabul.
The Afghan army and air force has not deserted,
As the media predicted,
But have inflicted 10,000 fatalities
To the contra merchantries.
This failure has been blamed on the ISI,
The Pakistani intelligence agency.pp
The Bush administration has chosen
To increase military aid to the contras,
While the Afghan government stability
And prestige grows every day
Even in the contra controlled
Refugee camps.

THE GERMAN DEMOCRATIC REPUBLIC
IS ON THE MOVE

A revolutionary popular movement
    Has set in motion a process
        Of sweeping changes.

    The renewal of socialism is on the agenda.
      It took peaceful mass protest of the people,
Demonstration of will by many
      Political organizations,
    Constructive efforts by dignitaries and
      Members of the churches and
    Increasing grassroots pressure within
Our own Party as well as a learning process
      In Party leadership to break up
    Rigid political structures and take
      The first steps of political change.

Radical reforms are inevitable.
      They have to serve workers,
Farmers, intellectuals and all other working people.
    The objective is to impart a new dynamism
To socialism by way of more democracy.
      For the reform of political system
        We propose that the elections
To the People's Chamber be held on
    The basis of a new electoral law.

We support an electoral law that guarantees
　　　Free, general and democratic elections
By secret ballot and ensures public control
　　　At all stages of the procedures.

We suggest that the People's Chamber and
　　　All local elected assemblies' exercise
Their constitutional rights and duties
　　　Without tutelage and restrictions
As sovereign bodies accountable to the people.
　　　We are in favor of a democratic coalition
　　　　　Government,
For a socialist constitutional state.
Our state is a constitutional state which is built
　　　On fundamental human rights an
Which organizes society in all spheres
　　　On the basis of law.
Law and justice are the yardsticks
　　　for the political activity of SUPG.
The SUPG purposes the establishment
　　　Of a constitutional court to monitor
Compliance with the constitution.
The Central Committee considers that
　　　The following laws are urgently required:
　　　A law on the freedom of assembly
　　　A law on the freedom of association
　　　An electoral law
　　　A law on the media
　　　A revision of the criminal law

Strict observance of the independence
        Of the judiciary is of particular importance.

Milos Jakes, general secretary of the Communist
        Party of Czechoslovakia resigned,
    As a result of mass demonstrations,
        And was replaced by Karel Urbanek.
The opposition Civic Forum announced
        It was calling off all strikes,
    And demonstrations following a meeting
        Tuesday with Premier Ladislav Adamec.
    Marian Calfa, minister for legal affairs,
Told reporters after the Adamic-Civic Forum
        Meeting that the government will ask
    Parliament to eliminate three articles
        Of the constitution:
    Those guaranteeing the CPC the leading role
        In political life, requiring a Marxist-Leninist
    Educational system and outlawing groups
    Not part of overall National Front organization.
        Czechoslovak Premier Ladislav Adamec
        Resigned Thursday after opposition groups
Failed to accept his latest proposal for broadening
        The government to include non-communist.
            He was replaced by
        Deputy Premier Marian Calfa,
    Who will continue negotiations
            For new cabinet.

Late Wednesday Manfred Gerlach,
A member of the Liberal Party and
Deputy chair of the Defense Council,
Was named acting GDR head of state
Following Egon Krenz' resignation
Wednesday.
Gerlach is the first head of state that
does not belong to Socialist Unity Party.
'The situation in the country and in the Party
Called for holding this extraordinary
Party Congress and convening it early.
The Party needs leadership in order to counteract
Signs of disintegration and
To restore its ability to act.'
Gregor Gysi said, the newly elected chair
Of the SUP.

'Administrative, centralized socialism
Participated a political, ecological and
Economic crisis,
Together with corruption and misuse of offices.
As in other socialist countries, it has proven
To be incapable of making a effective
Contribution to the solution
Of the problems confronting all humanity.'
Gregor Gysi acknowledged that because
Of the personal experiences,
Many citizens of the GDR are looking
To the FGR as a model.

He expressed appreciation of the progress
Made by the working people of FGR.

'But, at the same time, we must not overlook
How limited these achievements are,
As democratic forces in those countries
Themselves point out.
The mentioned achievements are limited
By the power interest of capitalist monopolies,
Especially international corporations
And the international military-industrial complex.
It is at that point that the sovereignty
Of the FRG in relation to the United States
And NATO comes to an end.'
'An expanding capitalist world market may appear,
At first sight, attractive to someone who has
Been used to a bureaucratically planned
Economic mismanagement.
But in its monopolistic form it also exacerbates
Existing global problems concerning
The protection of the environment,
The safeguarding of peace and the potential
For social-economic development.
Indeed, it leads to mass unemployment,
Fear of life, socially unjust society
Which has written off one-third of its people
And, of course, to growing misery
In poorer countries.'

We are not permitted to gamble away
    The democratic beginnings and
Self-determination of the people of the GDR.
And we would be doing just that if we allowed
    The polit-bureaucratic to be followed
By the rule of capitalist magnates.'

'The crisis of administrative-centralized socialism
    In our country can be resolved only
If the GDR follows a third path,
    Going beyond Stalinist socialism and
The rule of transnational monopolies in that
    Respect we owe a particular obligation
        To the social interest of our people.'
'Our fundamental values are solitary
    In the development of all,
        Equal opportunities for individual
Self-realization, and safeguarding
Of the environmental and cultural heritage
        Of humankind, all based on
Individual freedom and basic rights.

A new Czechoslovak government
        Of 'national understanding'
    Was sworn in Sunday by President Husak,
Who resigned after the ceremony.

The government is headed by Prime Minister
Marian Calfa, a 43-year-old lawyer
And Communist Party member.
Its 21 members include a total of ten Communist,
Two members of each from Socialist and
People's Parties, historically allied
With the Communist Party,
and seven independents.
Four of the seven are leading members
Of the Civic Forum or
The Public Against Violence,
The principle Czech and Slovak
Opposition movements.
At a news conference Sunday, Calfa said
The new government's responsibility
Would be to prepare for parliamentary
Elections as soon as possible,
Probably by the end of June.
He referred to stepped-up economic change,
Including 'radical reforms
To lead out of stagnation,'
And said measures to ensure
Economic equilibrium
Were being worked out by a team
Of Communist economic heads
By the First Deputy Prime Minister
Walter Komarek

Calfa pledged that his government would
'respect all foreign commitments.'
Including Czechoslovakia's participation
In Warsaw Treaty Organization,
And would seek 'to contribute to European
Integration.'

PRESIDENT NICOLAE CEAUSESCU, WAS EXECUTED
ON DECEMBER 25, 1989, BY A MILITARY TRIBUNAL.
THE DEATH OF INNOCENT VICTIMS, IN ARMED ATTACKS
AGAINST THE PEOPLE'S REBELLION CAME TO A HALT.
A COUNCIL OF NATIONAL SALVATION IS FUNCTIONING
TO RESTORE ORDER. THE COUNCIL HAS CALLED FOR A
RETURN TO WORK AND PREPATIONS FOR ELECTIONS
IN ROMANIA IN APRIL.
A decrease on production between 1980 and 1988,
The real gross national product went up
3 percent per year, which is less than average
Rate of previous decades ---
3.3, 3.8, 2.8 percent respectively.
The percentage rise in employment was higher
Between 1971 and 1978 (20 percent),
And the numerical and percentage increases
Were several times more in China.
The percentage increase was greater
In a number of countries.
Official U. S. statistics show that between

1980 and 1988, employment rose
15.6 million, or 16 percent.
During the previous eight years, it went up
17.2 million or 21 percent.
In the Reagan years, manufacturing production
Worker's employment, providing
Relatively higher-paying jobs,
Fell 7 percent from an already depressed level.
Real weekly earning of all private industry
Non-super-visionary workers
Declined by 3 percent over the eight
Reagan years,
That continued in 1989 to a November level
17 percent below the 1972 peak.
The latest unemployment rate of 5.4 percent
Is above the rate in most pre-Reagan
Post-war years.
The actual average rate during his eight years,
7.5 percent, exceeding 6.5 percent
During the Carter's four years in office
And was much higher than during
Earlier postwar administrations.

In Cuba, we are engaged in a process of rectification.
No revolution or truly socialist rectification
Is possible without a strong,
Disciplined respected Party.
Such a process cannot be advanced

By slandering socialism,
                    Destroying its values,
                Casting slurs on the Party,
        Demoralizing its vanguard,
                Abandoning the Party's role,
        Eliminating socialist discipline and
    Sowing chaos and anarchy everywhere.
                This may foster a counterrevolution
    But not revolutionary changes.' (Fidel Castro)

There has been a long-term communication gap
        Between the leadership and
                    the membership and grassroots.
    The leadership was unaware
                    of the mass thought patterns.
            They did not know the nature
        of the people's complaints and criticisms.
            They were isolated, both physically
                        And politically.

During the Reagan years public housing units
        Under construction at all levels
                Of government dropped 51,000
                    In 1981 to 9,500 in 1987.
    Between 1981 and 1989, real per capita
        Federal outlays for community and
    Regional development declined 60 percent.
                For education employment training

And social services 38 percent,
And for income security by 9 percent.
Aid to the state and local governments declined
13 percent and the share of state and
Local capital outlays covered by federal grants
Went down from 36 to 26 percent.
A valid appraisal would find an increase
Of those living in poverty from 29.3 million,
Or 13 percent, in 1980
To 31.9 million, or 13.1 percent in 1988.
Today 9 million more people fell below
The poverty than at a post-war low point
In 1973.

Afro-American median household income fell
From 57.6 percent of white income
In 1980 to 57 percent in 1988.
There was a post-war record of bank failures
And foreclosures and complex domestic
And international financial crisis.
The international economic and financial position
Of the U.S. capital has worsened
In almost all aspects.
Social conditions deteriorated with
the emergence of large-scale homelessness,

The drastic serge in the number of children
in single-parent homes, the weakening
Of job safety and health enforcement,

Decay of the economic infrastructure
        Worsening of pollution.

Because of outstanding achievements
        In building socialism,
Party leadership developed attitudes
        Of complacency, smugness, elitism,
Bureaucratic and demagogic methods.
In most socialist development, developed out
        Of objective as well as subjective
        conditions. (Gus Hall, CPUSA)

THE EMERGENCE OF BILLIONARIES
AND RECORD BUSINESS PROFITS did not
Reflect the economic status of the majority.
Averaging the gains of the profit makers
With the pittance of the underpaid give
A totally distorted view of the actual situation.
        (Victor Perlo, Economic chair, CPUSA)

Today is July 22, 1990, and the time has come
To end this poem. The argument of poem
Has been achieved. I have reestablished
My existence. This may be viewed as of no
Significance, yet for myself it is a major
Accomplishment.

The young lady from Czechoslovakia,
With her colleague visited me for five days.
I have never had such a good time in my life.
I was a bit to serious since this visit was of
Importance. A new state of existence has been
Achieved. The many visits to Eastern Europe
May develop in to a healthy relationship.
I would like to establish a second home in Europe.

AGREEMENT OF A UNITED GERMANY ACHIEVED.

Helmut Kohl and Mikhail Gorbachev achieved
An agreement on Monday on reunification of
Germany. Gorbachev stated: 'We are leaving
One epoch in international relations, and entering
Another --- a period, I think, of strong, prolonged
Peace.' Kohl spoke that the German-Soviet treaty
Will be worked out 'for a long time ahead and
In good-neighborly spirit.'

A unified Germany may not decide which alliance
To join.
A unified Germany will not have nuclear, biological
Or chemical arms.
A unified Germany will be limited to 370,000 troops.

SOLIDARITY LEADER, LECH WALESA,
ENCOUNTERED RESISTANCE.
Supporters of presidential bid for Lech Walesa's
Met resistance.
The powerful Civic Committee defeated a resolution
To move ahead dates for a presidential and
Parliamentary elections. Premier Tadeus Mazowiecki
Endorsements continued to grow, as public opinion
Polls express that 50 percent reject the Nobel Prize
Winner's bid to end parliamentary debate and
Rule by decree in order to end delays.

President Wojciech Jaruszelski, former PUWP first
Secretary, stated in a television interview that
His presidency is a 'service role' and that he will
Leave 'when the time is recognized as proper
For a change.' He has won great respect, even
Among Solidarity activists.

WASHINGTON --- The Supreme Court Tuesday,
January 2, 1990, in 6-3 decreed, inmates,
Even before conviction to take mind-altering drugs.
Though this was the common practice in prisons
It now becomes the law. This ruling continues
The anti-human rights swing of the Reagan years.
Leonard Rubenstein, director of Mental Health
Law Project, said that there is a danger in the court's
Ruling on mind-altering drugs. While it is very clear

That the decision doesn't apply outside of prisons,
We anticipate that the people will try to apply it
That way,' he said. Rubenstein added, 'I am
Concerned that it can lead to more people taking
There medications if someone can come up with
A justification to it 'counterrevolution'.
Associate Justice John Stevens wrote in dissent
'The liberty interest of citizens to resist that the
Administration of mind-altering drugs arises from
Our nation's most basis values.'
Stevens argued, 'The mere fact a decision is made
By doctor does not make it certain that professional
Judgement in fact was exercised.'
Stevens said, 'so serving institutional conveniences
Eviscerates the inmate's substitutive liberty Interest
In the integrity of his body and mind. The case
Resulted from a lawsuit by Washington state prisoner
Walter Harper who said the drugs caused swelling of
His brain and induced catatonic-like states. He said
Among the other results of the drugs were hyper-
Tension, weird dreams, vomiting, headaches, muscle
Spasms and blurred vision.

250,000 GDR FARMERS DEMONSTRATE AGAINST
'PRICE' OF UNIFICATION.
Over 250,000 farmers and farm workers
demonstrated in Dresden, Halle, Gera, Rostock,
Erfurt, Suhl, and a dozen other towns.

50,000 demonstrate in the Alexanderplatz
In East Berlin threw vegetables and shouted down
East German officials.
This week the East German governing coalition
Collapsed. The Social Democrats withdrawal may
Prevent passage of the unity treaty with
West Germany.
'Is poverty the price of freedom?' 'No farmers,
No future.'

The slogan as East and West German agricultural
Workers presented demands to the West German
Government. The halt in the drop in prices, adequate
Export subsides and intervention to halt imposition
Of capitalist market policies.

70,000 RALLIES AGAINST 'ANNEXATION' OF THE GDR.

A rally called by the Party of Democratic Socialism
In Lustgarten provided a moment when
70,000 people could protest that the present
Agreement of unification is in reality 'annexation'
Of the GDR.
Speakers from the GDR, West Berlin, and the FDR
Announced a necessity of saving the advancements
Of socialism and to ensure a non-militarized
Germany.
The coalition of thousands of signatures demanding

The return radio station recently closed because of its
Left oreintation to young people.
The station was reopened.
Gregor Gysi, PDS chair, called for 'the coming
Together of the left-wing forces and the building of
United Socialist force.' 'I will vote in the Bundestag
Against and measure not in the interest of the people
of the GDR. You can't push aside 40 years of history
And gains of the German Democratic Republic.

Reference Books:

The Rise and Fall of the Third Reich
By William L. Shirer

The French Revolution 1787-1799
By Albert Soboul

The Deutsch Democratic Republic
Czechoslovak Socialist Republic
Government books

CPSIA information can be obtained
at www.ICGtesting.com
Printed in the USA
LVHW030357140423
744360LV00001B/152

9 781959 895350